Francis Ellingwood Abbot

The Way out of Agnosticism

Or, The Philosophy of free Religion

Francis Ellingwood Abbot

The Way out of Agnosticism
Or, The Philosophy of free Religion

ISBN/EAN: 9783337079710

Printed in Europe, USA, Canada, Australia, Japan

Cover: Foto ©ninafisch / pixelio.de

More available books at **www.hansebooks.com**

THE
WAY OUT OF AGNOSTICISM

OR THE

PHILOSOPHY OF FREE RELIGION

BY

FRANCIS ELLINGWOOD ABBOT, Ph.D.
LATE INSTRUCTOR IN PHILOSOPHY IN HARVARD UNIVERSITY

BOSTON
LITTLE, BROWN, AND COMPANY
1890

NOTE.

THE following papers (with the exception of the Introduction) are based on notes of forty-one lectures delivered in 1888, in the "Advanced Course, Philosophy 13," Harvard University. Originally published during the year 1889 as a series of contributions to a monthly periodical in Boston, they are now addressed, not to those who are impatient of serious thought or incapable of following a close and continuous argument, but to those (and their name is legion) who, though able and willing to think, have been distressed or dismayed by the seeming inability of theistic writers in this age to meet and defeat agnosticism on its own professed ground, — the ground of science and philosophy. By a wholly new line of reasoning, drawn exclusively from those sources, this book aims to show that, in order to refute agnosticism and establish enlightened theism, nothing is now necessary but to philosophize that very scientific method which agnosticism barbarously misunderstands and misuses. Of the success of the perhaps unwise attempt to show this in so small a compass, the educated public must be the judge. But it may be well to quote here these wise and true words of Arnold Toynbee, one of the noblest young men of the century, whose early death was a calamity to England and to the world : —

"Had liberal theologians in England combined more often with their undoubted courage and warmth definite philosophic views, religious liberalism would not now be condemned as offering nothing more than a mere sentiment of vague benevolence. Earnest and thoughtful people are willing to encounter the difficulty of mastering some unfamiliar phrases of technical language, when they find they are in possession of a sharply defined intellectual position upon which their religious faith may rest."

F. E. A.

CAMBRIDGE, MASS., Feb. 10, 1890.

INTRODUCTION.*

IN its relation to religion, the century now drawing to its close is emphatically the AGE of AGNOSTICISM. All the leaders of its characteristic thought have more or less consciously, more or less completely, broken with Christianity, — that is, broken with that venerable theory of the universe for which the Christian theology and the Christian church have definitely stood for nearly two thousand years. But these leaders are paralyzed when it comes to constructive thought. They have no other theory of the universe to propose; they aim at none; they agree, if they agree on anything, that no theory of the universe is possible. What is known as the "philosophy of evolution," certainly so far as its great champions and expounders are concerned, strictly limits itself to a mere knowledge of "phenomena," and strictly denies all possible knowledge of "noumena"; it formulates a mode of happening, a uniformity of process, a law of co-existence and sequence, but claims to demonstrate the impossibility of comprehending ultimate causes, or of arriving at any theory of the universe as an intelligible unity. Whether the phenomenal universe is the product of intelligence or of unintelligence,— whether the human being is a creative first cause or a mere link in an endless and eternal chain of effects, and whether his conscious existence ceases at death, or continues beyond the grave,— all these vital questions, fundamental to any real theory of the universe, it declares to be necessarily and absolutely unanswerable. God, Freedom, and Immortality, the supreme interests of human thought and human life alike,— these, to the evo-

---

* This Introduction appeared in THE NEW IDEAL for January, 1889, under the caption, "Creative Liberalism."

lution-philosophy in its present form, are insoluble problems, the eternal rock-barriers of the ever-restless ocean of human speculation. Every form of the evolution-philosophy which is founded on "the Unknowable" is founded on agnosticism, or denial of the possibility of any comprehensive theory of the universe; and agnosticism is the prevalent philosophy of liberalism in the nineteenth century.

This statement needs no proof, for it simply records a fact of observation, patent to every onlooker. A single significant illustration of it is enough.

The two most successful novels of the past summer hinge on the conflict between traditional Christianity and modern liberalism. In "Robert Elsmere" and in "John Ward, Preacher," portraits are painted of the modern liberal, as seen by keen-eyed observers; and in each case the liberal is an agnostic.

Says Robert Elsmere, only a few days before his death: "I often lie here, Flaxman, wondering at the way in which men become the slaves of some metaphysical word—*personality*, or *intelligence*, or what not! What meaning can they have as applied to *God?* Herbert Spencer is quite right. We no sooner attempt to define what we mean by a Personal God than we lose ourselves in labyrinths of language and logic. But why attempt it at all? I like that French saying: '*Quand on me demande ce que c'est que Dieu, je l'ignore; quand on ne me le demande pas, je le sais très-bien!*' No, we cannot realize Him in words—we can only live in Him, and die to Him!"

Helen Ward expresses no less clearly the same bewilderment and defeat of thought: "But, after all, this question of eternal punishment is such a little thing, so on the outside of the great puzzle! One goes in, and in: Why is sin, which is its own punishment, in the world at all? What does it all mean, anyhow? Where is God, and why does He let us suffer here, with no certainty of a life hereafter? Why does He make love and death in the same world? Oh, that is so cruel,—love and death together! Is He, at all? Those are the things, it seems to me, one has to think about. But why do I go over it all? We can't get away from it, can we?" And again: "To some of us God is only another name for the power of good,—or, one might as well say force, and that is blind and impersonal; there is nothing comforting or tender in the thought of force. How do you suppose the conviction of the personality of God is reached?" And once again, when, after the death of her beloved husband, a friend tries to comfort her by saying—"It is so much happier for him now; he must see so clearly; and the old grief is lost in joy,"—Helen answered wearily: "No, you must not say those things to me. I cannot feel them. I am glad he has no pain; in an eternal sleep there is at least no pain. But I must just wait my life out, Gifford. I cannot hope; I dare not. I could not go on living, if I thought he were living somewhere, and needing me. No, it is ended. I have had my life."

The deep pathos of these two noble works of fiction, far truer to life as it is than many so-called biographies, lies in the remorseless fidelity with which, perhaps unconsciously and unintentionally, they expose the intellectual beggarliness of liberalism in its present unfledged state. Such dearth of great ideas, such piteous poverty of comprehension, as is exhibited in the mental condition of these two typical liberals, simply shows that liberalism, so far as it claims to be the custodian of high truth, is to-day infinitely inferior to the Christian mythology which it has displaced. Periods of revolution are doubtless necessary, but only by way of transition to periods of higher construction; and, if liberalism could by any possibility fall permanently into the arrested development of agnosticism, it would be no heir of the future. Robert Elsmere and Helen Ward, lovely and noble as personal characters, represent, as agnostic thinkers, the lowest and crudest, because the least intellectual, type of liberalism. It is an awful tragedy of the human soul, when its holiest affections and impulses and aspirations, guided no longer by the ancient superstitions which, in whatever coarse and prickly envelope, contained nevertheless most precious *thoughts*, are bereft of all other guidance, gasping for life in the exhausted receiver of mere *vacuity of thought*.

This merely negative attitude of mind, this emptiness of all positive ideas respecting the supreme problems which man is set to solve, is indeed the present characteristic of liberalism, but only because liberalism is at the very beginning of its career. Agnosticism, in itself considered, is nothing but intellectual bewilderment, confusion of thought, a mere temporary defeat and despair of human reason in the presence of questions which it has not yet learned how to answer. When liberalism once comes to understand itself, — when it once discovers how to go to work, how to handle these questions, how to synthesize the facts and laws which modern science has established beyond reasonable doubt,— then it will see its way clear to a theory of the universe founded upon modern knowledge, and will no longer fancy its mission to mankind discharged by merely overthrowing a theory of the universe founded upon ancient superstition. The era of constructive or creative liberalism is fated to come; and what it will create is necessarily a new theory of the universe, without which no religious movement can live. The real moral of "Robert Elsmere" and "John Ward, Preacher," has been as yet drawn by no one; the real lesson of the helpless and hopeless liberalism they too justly depict is deeper than any of the critics have as yet perceived. Briefly put, it is this: *men must either learn to think more profoundly, or else unlearn to feel*.

That is the dilemma to which agnosticism reduces the human spirit. If all knowledge of God, Freedom, and

Immortality is impossible to man, the only escape from intolerable anguish, in the constant presence of pain and death, must lie in a stoical suppression of the power to feel — in a desperate resolve to think and feel no more, but to extinguish all deep thought and all high feeling through frantic self-absorption in the soulless details of life. Yet what an impossible escape! In every noble nature, deep thought and high feeling have become a necessity; the only possible escape for such lies in deeper thought and higher feeling. Here is revealed the supreme duty of modern liberalism to press resolutely forward, away from agnosticism, to a positive, scientific, all-comprehensive theory of the universe. It is infinitely false that such a theory is unattainable. The agnosticism which professes to prove its unattainability is nothing but one of two things — either intellectual imbecility or intellectual cowardice. The one unpardonable sin of the intellect is to despair of itself. Liberalism has always stood for *freedom* — freedom from dogma and freedom from ecclesiastical control. Well and good: let it always stand for that! But now it must stand for *truth as well*, and for the power of human reason to attain the truth. To liberalism alone can poor humanity, losing day by day its hold upon the Christian theory of the universe, look for a new theory that may guide its thought and life. The paramount duty of construction and creation to which liberalism is now called is that of working out such a theory, bravely, hopefully, patiently, reverently, devotedly; and THE NEW IDEAL will justify itself to the world, if it proves itself to be that *New Thought* which is the world's deepest and most imperative need.

THE PHILOSOPHY OF FREE RELIGION.

I.

It is with no little hesitation and reluctance that, yielding to the editor's urgency, I undertake the difficult task of attempting to write out, in as simple and untechnical a manner as the nature of the subject permits, an outline of the theory of the universe which, if I mistake not, lies latent and implicit in the scientific method, and which must become explicit, whenever this method shall be faithfully applied to the great problems of philosophy. The reasons why I should not undertake the task are numerous and formidable. First and foremost, perhaps, is the fact that, although the ground-plan of this theory is already thoroughly matured, the literary execution of it is as yet scarcely even begun, and from want of opportunity may never be completed; and it seems almost absurd to present the abridgment of a work which does not yet exist to be abridged. Next, the impossibility of doing justice to any philosophy by discarding its appropriate diction, suppressing its necessary subtilty of distinction, and curtailing its indispensable reasoning, renders such an attempt almost a crime against philosophic truth itself. Further, the fit place of publication would naturally be some journal specially devoted to philosophy, rather than a journal like The New Ideal, which does not address itself in particular to a philosophic audience. Again, the agnosticism so widely diffused among liberals at the present day makes me gravely doubt the utility of any such publication; the thought is suited to no self-satisfied ignorance, but to the determined, keen, hopeful spirit of investigation, to the spirit which counts present failure as only a stepping-stone to future success, to the spirit which is fixed, resolute, indomitable in the effort to wrest knowledge from Nature, and which repudiates the imbecile philosophy that founds itself upon "the Unknowable" and pretends to set up "limits of human knowledge" in a universe everywhere penetrable by patient and persistent reason; in short, it is not to those who believe a theory of the universe impossible, but to those who know that a sound theory of it is inevitable, whenever science ripens into philosophy, that I can look with any expectation of intelligent sympathy. Lastly, I am painfully aware that to state my results briefly and without due argumentation must subject me, however unanswerable and conclusive the necessarily omitted reasons for them may be, to groundless charges of assumption, presumption, dogmatism. These considerations (with others needless to mention) are quite sufficient to render the proposed undertaking anything but a source of pleasurable anticipation to myself.

Nevertheless, there are reasons on the other side which have led me to consent to make the attempt, whatever the consequences may prove to be. Chief among them is the wish to render some little help to the brave and devoted editor of THE NEW IDEAL, in whatever way he himself judges he most wants help, and to further as far as possible his bold enterprise of giving once more to liberalism a journal of high constructive aims and earnest helpfulness to man. Moreover, there is in my own mind a lurking hope that even now, scattered here and there, may be found spirits already eager to welcome the higher thought of the future, already prepared to demand an interpretation of the fact of Evolution which shall be freed from the humiliating and entangling alliance with phenomenism, agnosticism, or know-nothingism, and already ripe for the reception of a thoroughly free philosophy, at once grounded in science and culminating in the loftiest moral and religious ideals. To the young I look for such spirits as these, for in the young is the hope of the world. There is no possible redemption for mankind from the political, commercial, industrial, and social immoralities of the present, except in the speedy development of ideals which shall fire the souls of the rising generation to give battle to this hydra-headed monster of corruption, and fight it down in the power of the higher life; and the power of the higher life is the power of the higher thought. Here, in this crying need of a higher thought than agnosticism has ever given or can ever give, lies the necessity of a new, constructive, non-agnostic liberalism; and I cannot resist the call to do my little part in answering the deepest need of my own time.

So much for the reasons why I should gladly, yet must not, refuse the task now laid upon me.

In justice, however, to all concerned, let it be distinctly understood at the very outset that the theory of the universe now to be advanced, as the intellectual foundation of a NEW IDEAL OF LIBERALISM, claims no other support than its own inherent and evident truth. It does not claim to be the philosophy of THE NEW IDEAL or of its editor; no one is authorized to declare this except the editor himself, and he must not be held responsible for anything said in this series of papers, unless he himself sees fit to approve it explicitly in words of his own. It would be unfair and ungenerous to him, if, merely because he has urged me to write the series, I should allow it to be imagined that I am in any sense his authorized representative or spokesman; and it would be equally unjust to myself, to the depth and strength of my own convictions, if I should allow it to be imagined that this theory of the universe needs any other corroboration than manifest congruity with the facts of the universe itself.

Furthermore, in entitling these papers "The Philosophy of Free Religion," it must not be understood that I claim for them the sanction of the Free Religious Association, or of any of its officers or members. These must speak for themselves; I do not speak for them at all. But I do claim the right to call by that name the philosophy which, in my own mind, had begun to shape itself, and which, in the *Christian Examiner* of September, 1865, and March, 1866, had begun to utter itself, before the Free Religious Association was organized,—the philosophy which, substantially the same as now, though less matured in form, impelled me in 1867 to join in the founding of that Association,—the philosophy which impelled me in 1869 to become the editorial founder of "*The Index*, A Weekly Paper Devoted to Free Religion," in entire independence of the Free Religious Association,—the philosophy which impelled me in 1880 to procure the donation of *The Index* to the Free Religious Association by the Index Association,—and the philosophy which impelled me in 1886, in the last issue of *The Index* itself, to protest against the transfer of its "good-will" to a new journal which straightway justified the protest by devoting itself avowedly to "Monism and Agnosticism . . . as positive and negative aspects of the one and only rational scientific philosophy." The title of this series of articles seems to me appropriate because they aim to develop the philosophy which must (consciously or unconsciously) underlie any and every free religious movement or institution: namely, the philosophy which results from the faithful application of the scientific method to the universe as a whole. They aim to sketch this necessary philosophy, as a theory of the universe logically involved in the scientific method itself, but not yet historically evolved from it in the intellectual consciousness of the world; they cannot, therefore, claim to represent the present convictions of any one except the writer, but they do claim to indicate the *necessary philosophical goal* of the great movement of modern scientific thought. And by this claim they must stand or fall.

What remains of this first article of the series must be devoted to a concise statement of the *beginning* and the *end* of the road now opening before us, in order that the reader may know exactly what to expect.

I. *The universal results of the special sciences, including the method common to them all, are the only possible data of philosophy or universal science.*
This principle, which alone can give to universal human reason a firm foothold in reality as universal human experience, is the necessary beginning-point of all philosophy which deserves to be called scientific. It means that philosophy cannot begin until the innumerable individuals of the human race have accumulated a common stock, great or small, of universal knowledge which has been proved, tested, or verified by their universal experience, and from which all the errors of individuals have been eliminated. It means that this common stock of verified knowledge of the universe, gained through long ages of experience and clarified by science, is the only solid ground of reality upon which philosophy can build; and that the only legitimate business of philosophy is to organize, systemize, and make the most of this universally verified knowledge — to combine the fragmentary and disconnected data of the special sciences in such a way as to unite them in one harmonious, comprehensive, and trustworthy theory of the universe as a whole.

II. *The universe is known as at once infinite machine, infinite organism, and infinite person — as mechanical in its apparent form and action, organic in its essential constitution, and personal in its innermost being: it is the eternally self-evolving and self-involving unity of the Absolute Real and the Absolute Ideal in* GOD.

This principle, which alone can give to universal human experience an intelligible unity in universal human reason, is the necessary end or outcome of all philosophy which deserves to be called scientific. It means that philosophy cannot end in the Infinite Impersonal without stultifying reason and experience at once,—that the Infinite Impersonal is below even the Finite Personal, and immeasurably below the Infinite All-Person,—that the Infinite Super-personal (or unknown and transcendent God) must include the Infinite All-Person (or known and immanent God), precisely as this includes the infinite organism and the infinite machine,—that the Infinite Impersonal can only be the false dream of an Infinite Sub-personal,—and that to identify a universe containing finite personalities with an Infinite Sub-personal is to wreck all possibility of conceiving Being as One, by making its oneness a self-contradictory thought. In other words, Infinite Impersonal Being is an impossible conception which never has been, and never can be, *thought* by any one; to think Infinite Being, however, is the necessity of all philosophy, and it can only be thought as at once infinitely mechanical, infinitely organic, and infinitely personal.

III. *The universe itself, as eternally self-evolving and self-involving unity of the Absolute Real and the Absolute Ideal in God, is the Ethical Realization of the* INFINITE DIVINE IDEAL, *which reflects itself in the* FINITE HUMAN IDEAL *as the sun reflects itself in the dew-drop; and the splendor of its reflection is proportioned to the intelligent, free, loyal, and loving obedience of the human soul to it, as at once the supreme law of Human Nature and the supreme known law of Universal Nature.*

This principle is the only one which can give universal and necessary objective validity to the Moral Law, kindle such an "enthusiasm of humanity" as shall illumine both the inner and the outer life with divine radiance, or furnish an adequate and indestructible foundation either to Ethics or to Religion; and it can only be derived from the theory of the universe which has been indicated above. These papers aim to trace the main lines of rational connection between the *beginning* and the *end* of this Philosophy of Free Religion, and thereby help to lay solid intellectual foundations for a new and true Ideal of Humanity — in the conviction that no ideal can ever become practicable, unless it first becomes comprehensible.

II.

§ 1. The foundation or beginning-point of all genuinely scientific philosophy, as already intimated, is the principle that *the universal results of the special sciences, including the method common to them all, are the only possible data of philosophy as universal science.*

In other words, philosophy cannot begin by throwing away the vast treasure of universal human knowledge, gathered by the coöperative and long-continued experience of mankind, in order to construct it afresh from the sole standpoint of individual consciousness. Such a reconstruction is impossible without using, in the very process itself, that knowledge which the individual has previously learned from others, from mankind; it is, therefore, a manifest, undeniable, and philosophically fatal "begging of the question." For this reason (not to mention many others for which here there is no room), the famous formula of Descartes, "I think, therefore I am," recognized by all competent writers as the foundation of so-called modern philosophy, represents a beginning-point which does not really begin; the very words in which it is expressed, and without which it could not be clearly thought at all, whether French, Latin, or English, were learned from others, and transmit knowledge to the individual which he tries in vain to sweep from his own mind, in order to make a fresh beginning from his immediate self-consciousness and philosophize without the necessity of acknowledging indebtedness to his fellow-men. The common experience of mankind has accumulated an immense fund of common knowledge, which enters more or less into the education of every individual; he spends years in learning this before he can possibly begin to philosophize on his own account, and is never able to separate it wholly from what he acquires through his independent activity. "Common sense" designates the *crude* mass of this common knowledge, mixed with much error; "science," in the form of numerous special sciences which sift out the error, establish the truth, and make fresh discoveries, each in the special direction of its own limited line of investigation, designates the *purified* mass of this common knowledge, freed from the crudities of "common sense," but left still in a disjointed and unorganized condition; "philosophy," just so far as it deserves its name, designates that more profound and comprehensive thinking which combines the fragmentary data of all the special sciences, blends them into one rational whole, and constitutes the *organized* mass of this common knowledge, freed not only from the crudities of "common sense," but also from the fragmentariness, half-views, and inevitable limitations of "science" itself. In other words, "common sense" studies the universe, but only with reference to the immediate needs of practical life; "science" studies it with reference to the needs of exact knowledge, but only in arbitrarily limited fields, provinces, or parts; "philosophy" studies it in its wholeness, totality, or unity, not only with reference to the needs of exact knowledge (universal science), but also with reference to those of practical life (ethics). Hence no individual can possibly limit the foundation of philosophy to the mere data of his own immediate consciousness, since these are themselves founded on the data of "common sense" and "science" alike, and presuppose that common knowledge which he has previously more or less learned from the human race in general. There is no help for it: philosophy must begin by taking the existence and reality of UNIVERSAL HUMAN KNOWLEDGE as its own given fact, datum, material, subject-matter, foundation,— or it can never begin at all.

§ 2. But where is this universal human knowledge stored? Where is it to be found? Where does it exist as a concrete reality? For, if philosophy founds upon a mere abstraction, it will itself be a mere abstraction in the end.

Universal human knowledge exists in UNIVERSAL LITERATURE, using the term in a sense so broad as to include every permanent record or register of human thought. It is only through *communication* (that is, the "making common") that individual knowledge enters into, or adds to, the great stock of common knowledge, and thereby universalizes itself in a true sense. Uncommunicated individual knowledge perishes with the individual; only communicated knowledge can become general or universal. Not all literature is knowledge; all completely universalized knowledge, however, derives its universality from its incorporation into literature, and exists in literature alone. For literature, in its essence, is not the mere material instruments of communication, but rather the *meaning* which was originally put into these things by living intelligences, and which, if it had not been put into them, could never be extracted from them by other living intelligences. It is not true that the reader gets from a book only what he himself freely constructs in the reading by the activity of his own mind. Not a little trash of this sort has been said and printed; but whoever receives a letter from a distant friend may easily know, if he will, that he receives from it *information or knowledge* which he himself could not possibly have originated or constructed in his own mind. Universal literature is, so to speak, the whole mass of letters or extant correspondence which has been bequeathed by the past to the present; it constitutes now the capitalized knowledge of the human race, and grows in bulk from age to age by the additions of each new generation. It consists, not in parchment or paper as such, but in the essential meaning, the objective thought, the new grouping of old symbols so as to make them express new ideas, which originated in the mind of the writer, and now reaches the mind of the reader through these outward signs alone. The medium is material, but the message is intellectual. This is the true "telepathy" (not a whit less wonderful because it is a fact of commonest experience), by which *human consciousness communicates with human consciousness through that which is not human consciousness.* The meaning communicated must pass through some material medium, vehicle, or bearer, or it could never be communicated at all; and the bearer of universal human knowledge, that is, the total message which man in the past has sent to man in the present, is universal literature.

§ 3. Now universal literature, being that by which alone human knowledge can completely universalize itself, depends upon UNIVERSAL LANGUAGE, as a world-wide fact. The plurality of languages in no wise obscures this fact. There is a universal grammar which finds in every language universal parts of speech, universal modes of combining them in judgments or universal propositions, and universal elements of the latter in UNIVERSAL TERMS. Every word, in every language, no matter what may be its grammatical function, is essentially and necessarily a universal term; that is, it must be of universal application, or it would be utterly useless as a word.

§ 4. Thus we find that the universal human knowledge which supplies to philosophy its only possible datum, subject-matter, or foundation, is all contained in universal literature, or, in the last analysis, in universal terms. The results of science must be permanently stored in this form, and can only be found in this form. Museums, laboratories, observatories, and all other machinery of science, are only so many feeders of literature, and exist for the sake of libraries, as so many treasure-houses of human discovery, study, thought; and all the libraries in the world, considered in their essence, are only a vast mass of universal terms. Hence philosophy cannot take the first step towards comprehension of the results of science, or of the method which has produced them, without first comprehending what universal terms really are; and the actual underpinning of every possible philosophy, whether the fact is admitted or not, consists in its consciously or unconsciously adopted doctrine of universal terms — in its THEORY OF UNIVERSALS. So much penetration as it shows in its Theory of Universals, so much, and no more, will it show in its interpretation of the Scientific Method, and this will exactly measure its worth to mankind in all time to come. In truth, the Scientific Method involves the Scientific Theory of Universals, and the Scientific Theory of Universals involves the Scientific Method; and henceforth philosophy has no legitimate business whatever except to interpret more profoundly, develop more highly, and apply more searchingly, rigorously, and universally, that perfect method of science by which man has mastered all he really knows of the universe he inhabits. The first great task of philosophy, then, is to lay deep and solid foundations for the expansion and ideal perfection of human knowledge in a bold, new, and true Theory of Universals. For so-called modern philosophy rests complacently in a Theory of Universals which is thoroughly mediæval or antiquated, and shows itself daily more and more powerless to construct a theory of the universe tenable in the light of modern knowledge. There is no room here for any criticism of the past, or even of any adequate exposition of the Scientific Theory of Universals itself; but it is necessary to make a compact statement which shall give at least a glimpse of its three chief aspects.

§ 5. The first form of the Universal is the universal term or WORD. A few primitive words, radicals, or roots, at first used indiscriminately, gradually developed into distinct parts of speech, and through phonetic modification, addition of prefixes or suffixes, composition, or other modes of internal or external change, gave rise at last to the numberless words of existing languages, the relations and affiliations of which are studied by comparative philology. Every word has its own genealogy, reaching far back into pre-historic ages; it lives a universal life quite independent of the individuals who successively use it, and constitutes a permanent organic product of a permanent organic community of speaking beings. Its universal life lies in its universal use by the community, to express some constant, or imperceptibly changing, universal meaning.

§ 6. The second form of the Universal is the universal meaning, conception, or CONCEPT. Just as all speaking is only a combination of words into sentences, so all thinking is only a combination of concepts into judgments or propositions. The concept is a permanently organized and growing thought, entering into countless judgments formed by the individual mind, yet always retaining substantially the same organic form. This permanent organic constitution of the concept, quite independent of the individual minds which successively form and use it, is the most significant fact about it; for the permanent and independent constitution of concepts alone explains the permanence and independence of words, as bearers of common concepts of the race, and demonstrates an ultimate origin of the concept which is independent of any and every individual as such. Every concept lives a universal life in the individual mind, appearing and re-appearing as a fixed or constant element in conscious thinking; its universal life lies in its universal use by the individual mind, as the essential meaning of its corresponding word; and this essential meaning is necessarily determined by the nature of the *what-is-meant*.

§ 7. The third form of the Universal is the universal *what-is-meant:* that is, the universal classes or kinds of things, the universal genera and species under which all known existences are discovered by science, or, in one word, the GENUS. Here we come to the very bottom of all philosophical analysis. Science claims to know real existences, to declare their real classes or kinds, and, at least to some extent, to explain their real mutual relations, interactions, and affiliations. The total results of all the special sciences may be summed up in two words: classification and genesis. Indeed, the one word classification suffices, for genesis means only the derivation of class from class, or kind from kind. Nothing is known by itself alone; it is known only through its kind. The essential constitution of every genus is that of *many things in one kind, one kind in many things:* the unity and the multiplicity are known inseparably together. Hence the genus is in no sense an abstraction, but the concrete totality of many realities in one reality; and this essentially organic constitution of the genus is the universal *what-is-meant* of the concept, just as the concept is the universal *meaning* of the word. Science itself may be defined as KNOWLEDGE OF THE GENUS: that is, knowledge of the universe, as the highest kind which includes all other kinds.

§ 8. Thus the genus is the universal kind; the concept is the universal thought of the universal kind; the word is the universal expression of the universal thought of the universal kind. There are here three distinct grades, or ascending orders, of universality: objective universality in the genus, subjective universality in the concept, and objective-subjective universality in the word. To borrow the terms of mathematics, the genus is a universal of the first power, the concept a universal of the second power, and the word a universal of the third power; and, just as the cube and the square of any quantity presuppose the first power, so the word and the concept presuppose the genus. The word speaks the concept, and the concept thinks the genus;

at the bottom of all, conditioning the very possibility of concept and word, lies the genus, as the only possible unit of known existence. If science is not the knowledge of objectively real genera or kinds, then there is no real knowledge, and a philosophy of the universe is impossible. But, if science is indeed such knowledge, then the *Scientific Theory of Universals* (here scarcely more than hinted at) is the *Atomic Theory of Philosophy;* and the GENUS, the CONCEPT, and the WORD are the ULTIMATE MOLECULES OF UNIVERSAL HUMAN KNOWLEDGE.

III.

§ 9. THE importance of the Theory of Universals in the past, present and future development of philosophic thought cannot be overstated. Every philosophy has grown out of some form of this theory, consciously adopted or unconsciously inherited, as its very life-germ; and every philosophy must follow out the line of development which its own peculiar form of the theory marks out for it beforehand. The character of its Theory of Universals moulds, controls, and predetermines the character of its Theory of Knowledge and its Theory of Being; and it is the union or fusion of these three theories in one comprehensive whole which constitutes a philosophy. Ignoring, therefore, all minor distinctions, it is necessary at least to glance at three great and fundamentally different forms of the Theory of Universals, which for convenience may be styled the Greek, the German, and the American.

§ 10. The Greek theory recognizes the UNIVERSAL in its threefold reality as the GENUS, the CONCEPT, and the WORD, although without sufficiently distinguishing these one from another. It teaches that the Individual Thing is alone real, as the unit of existence and of knowledge alike; but it also teaches that the Universal, as sum of all the real characteristics or marks which are common to all things of one kind, exists whole and entire in each individual thing of that kind, and alone constitutes its intelligible reality as a fact in Nature. This is at least to conceive the Genus as depending on man neither for its existence nor for its intelligibility,— as being the real intelligible essence of the individual thing in itself, and, as such, an ultimate origin of the Concept and the Word. Hence this undeveloped

Greek theory, teaching the *Reality of the Universal in the Individual Thing*, has been for centuries fittingly denominated REALISM.

§ 11. The German theory recognizes the Universal as the Concept and the Word, but denies it altogether as the Genus, — denies it, that is, as a reality in a real Nature known by Man, yet independent of him. It teaches that the Individual Thing in Nature, even if it exists, cannot be known either in itself or in any of its real relations, internal or external. It teaches that the Universal is absolutely nothing but the work of human reason, has no real existence except as the Concept and the Word, and, as such, has nothing to do with individual things in themselves, which cannot possibly be known to exist. It teaches that the Concept and the Word have no ultimate origin but Man, and that the notion of real intelligible genera in Nature, existing independently of Man, is a monstrous fiction of mere untutored imagination or "common sense." Hence the German theory, teaching the *Mere Ideality of the Universal in the Concept and the Word*, completely extinguishes, merges, or absorbs the Genus in the Concept or Idea, and has long been fittingly denominated CONCEPTUALISM or IDEALISM.

In this German theory of Universals lies the deep, secret, and generally unsuspected source of all modern AGNOSTICISM, a result which was uncritically accepted, ready-made, by Spencer and Huxley from Hamilton and Mansel, borrowed by Hamilton and Mansel from Kant and the post-Kantian Idealists, and originally developed by Kant out of Hume and other adherents of Scholastic Nominalism.

§ 12. The American or Scientific Theory of Universals, like the Greek theory, recognizes the Universal in its threefold reality, but in a much fuller, higher, and profounder sense. The Word is the UNIVERSAL OF SPEECH; the Concept is the UNIVERSAL OF THOUGHT; the Genus is the UNIVERSAL OF BEING. The Word speaks the Concept, and the Concept thinks the Genus; the content or meaning of the Word is identical with the constitution of the Concept, and the constitution of the Concept (provided this be verifiable or scientifically true) is identical, so far as it goes, with the constitution of the Genus. The Genus itself is not a mere sum of characteristics or marks common to all things of one kind, and therefore real in a lower sense than the things themselves; on the contrary, it is *the self-related organic whole of many real things in one real kind,* and therefore precisely as real or concrete as they. So defined, the Genus, or Universal of Being, and not the Individual Thing as such, is alone real. It alone is the real unit of all known existence, and therefore constitutes an indispensable co-factor with the understanding in originating the Concept and the Word; while the individual thing can neither exist nor be known out of necessary relation to its kind, but can exist and be known only in, with, and through its kind, which, again, can exist and be known only in, with, and through a higher kind. What is known through the Concept and the Word is never the *independent, isolated, or unrelated thing,* nor yet the *common essence of many unrelated things as a mere abstraction,* but always the *concrete kind of many interrelated things as one self-related reality.* Hence it is not true, as the Greek theory teaches, that the Universal exists whole and entire in *each individual* of the same kind; on the contrary, it exists only in *all the individuals* of that kind, as necessarily united in the Genus or Universal of Being. Neither is it true, as the German theory teaches, that the Universal has no real or intelligible existence in things in themselves, that is, in Nature as a reality independent of Man; for this is to deny the very possibility of science, as verified knowledge of such real Nature. Hence the American theory, teaching the *Reality of the Universal in the Concrete Kind or Genus, as the Sole Object of the Scientific Concept and Sole Meaning of the Scientific*

Word, and thereby preserving all the truth, while correcting the errors, of both Greek and German theories, is fittingly denominated SCIENTIFIC REALISM.

§ 13. These three fundamental forms of the Theory of Universals, therefore, may be shortly contrasted as follows:—

I. The Greek theory teaches that the Individual Thing-in-itself is the ultimate reality, but that the Universal is also real, in a lower sense, as the known essence of the Individual Thing-in-itself.

II. The German theory denies that the Individual Thing-in-itself is known at all, and teaches that the Universal is real only in the Concept and the Word.

III. The American theory teaches that the Universal is equally real in the Word, the Concept, and the Genus; and that the Individual Thing and the Universal Kind are known, each *in* and *with* and *through* the other, in the GENUS-IN-ITSELF. The Word, the Concept, and the Genus are the ultimate molecules of universal human knowledge; and universal human knowledge itself, in its purified form as science, is all reducible in the last analysis to KNOWLEDGE OF THE GENUS,—that is, to knowledge of the innumerable genera, classes, or kinds of existence which together constitute the Universe or Highest Kind (*summum genus*).

Thus each of the three theories determines in a different way the OBJECT OF KNOWLEDGE, and thereby predetermines a different THEORY OF KNOWLEDGE and THEORY OF BEING. To the Greek theory, the sole object of knowledge is *the Universal in the Individual Thing*. To the German theory, the sole object of knowledge is *the Universal in the Concept or Idea*. To the American theory, the sole object of knowledge is *the Universal Kind and the Individual Thing as necessarily correlated in the* REAL GENUS-IN-ITSELF.

§ 14. For all present purposes, it must suffice to exhibit,

without criticism or argument, these three theories side by side, and leave the thoughtful reader to be arguer or critic for himself. The American or Scientific Theory of Universals underlies and supports the whole fabric of modern science. Science presents itself as exact and verified knowledge of genera, classes, or kinds of real existence, at all times observable and verifiable in the Universe as the supreme Genus. This knowledge embraces a vast body of scientific concepts, expressed in scientific words; and the truth of each concept depends absolutely on the identity of its constitution, so far as it goes, with that of the genus which is its correlate or object.

§ 15. But the identity of constitution between a subjective concept and an objective genus requires that there should be something in common between thoughts and things — something which may exist indifferently in either. Such a common term is found in the INHERENT SYSTEM OF RELATIONS or IMMANENT RELATIONAL CONSTITUTION; for relations may subsist indifferently between things or between thoughts, and therefore be the same in both. For instance, the relation or ratio between the circumference and diameter of a circle chalked on a blackboard is precisely the same as the relation or ratio between the circumference and diameter of a circle conceived in imagination: both relations inhere necessarily in the constitution of the circle as a circle, wherever found, and are necessarily identical. In other words, equal ratios are one and the same ratio. Aristotle recognized the truth of this principle unequivocally two thousand years ago, when he said that, in such cases, "equality is unity." If this principle is true, then the immanent relational constitution of a concept may be strictly and absolutely identical, so far as it goes, with the immanent relational constitution of a genus.

§ 16. The Scientific Theory of Universals, therefore, which science presupposes in every statement of cosmical fact or cosmical law, necessarily involves the great, profound, and all-embracing principle of the OBJECTIVITY OF RELATIONS: namely, the principle that *relations are no less real, discoverable, verifiable, and intelligible in the objective world than they are in subjective thought.* The real object of every scientific concept is a self-related genus in Nature; and the possibility of observing and verifying it is the absolute condition of the possibility of science. The whole business of science is to observe, verify, and understand real genera in Nature, — that is, to discover them; it does not attempt the impossible task of proving the possibility of its own discovery, since every such proof is a manifest begging of the question. The only philosophy, therefore, which either does or can harmonize itself with science is that which defends the discoverability of real genera in Nature, or (what is the same thing precisely) recognizes *objective generic relations as the intelligible essence of a real environment not dependent on man either for its existence or for its intelligibility.* Such a philosophy is that which founds upon Scientific Realism, as opposed to Philosophical Idealism; and no other can justly lay claim to the epithet "modern."

§ 17. No philosophy, it is true, can demonstrate by pure reasoning that the Genus exists, since all reasoning, however pure, assumes the existence of the Genus. But science has already demonstrated its existence in the only possible way, not by pure reasoning, but by observation and verification. If observation and verification cannot demonstrate the real existence of the Genus, philosophy itself, in any sane sense of the word, is annihilated; for philosophy has nothing to work with except concepts, and, since concepts can think nothing whatever but genera, the doubt or denial of genera is the destruction of all concepts themselves. The legitimate work of philosophy is to take from science the concepts it has already acquired by scientific observation and verification, to combine them in new and higher concepts through philosophic hypothesis, and to confirm philosophic hypothesis by philosophic verification, — in a word, to discover still larger genera than are presented in the limited fields of investigation of the special sciences, and thereby to increase knowledge of the whole real universe. Philosophy, in truth, is only the completion or higher evolution of science itself, and can never attain to any *higher kind of certitude* than that to which science has already attained. This recognition of the results of science as the foundation of philosophy is not to "beg the question," "take the universe for granted," or "build on mere baseless assumption"; for the existence of the Genus has been long ago demonstrated by science in the only possible way, to wit, by observation and verification. The sole "postulate" of philosophy is the TRUTH OF SCIENCE — which is disputable by no educated man; and, at bottom, the truth of science is the truth of the Scientific Theory of Universals.

IV.

§ 18. It has been thus far shown that the real object of knowledge is not, as the Greek Theory of Universals teaches, the "tode ti" or INDIVIDUAL OBJECTIVE THING-IN-ITSELF; nor yet, as the German Theory teaches, the "Vorstellung" or UNIVERSAL SUBJECTIVE CONCEPT-IN-ITSELF; but rather, as the American or Scientific Theory teaches, the UNIVERSAL OBJECTIVE GENUS-IN-ITSELF. That is to say, the real object of knowledge is not the concept at all (though this, too, may become a real object of knowledge), but that which is really known by means of the concept: namely, the REAL UNIVERSAL KIND OF REAL INDIVIDUAL THINGS, internally so self-related as to constitute one essential whole out of many essential parts, and rendered intelligible through this real internal self-relation.

§ 19. Against this determination of the object of knowledge may be arrayed the current notions of the "relativity of knowledge." This doctrine, a truism or a falsity according as it is conceived, is too often made to take account only of the cognitive relation between the object and the subject, ignoring altogether the internal self-relatedness of the object in itself — which is the main part of the business. The argument commonly founded on it is that, since the object can only be known in relation to the subject, and since man's knowing-faculty is necessarily limited and imperfect, therefore *man can know nothing of the object as it is in itself.* This conclusion is far too large for the premises. From these it only follows that man's knowledge of the object is limited and imperfect — which is true; it does not follow that man knows nothing of the object as it is in itself — which is false. The above conclusion makes two enormous assumptions: that the object *as known* must of necessity be totally different from the object *as it is in itself*, and that the object as it is in itself cannot be known *at all*, unless it is known *wholly*. Neither of these assumptions has any foundation in reason or in fact. Just so far as man discovers the real internal self-relatedness of the object, just so far he knows it as it is in itself; for to know it " in itself" can only mean to know it in its internal relations. Science, which is his verified knowledge both of external and internal relations of the object, is at once the measure and the proof of his knowledge of it as it is in itself.

Rationally interpreted, the doctrine of the "relativity of knowledge" means merely that man can know the object so far only as he has the capacity to know it — which is surely a very innocent proposition; but to interpret it as meaning that man cannot at all know the object as it is in itself is to commit the absurdity of denying the very possibility of human knowledge. For "not to know the object as it is in itself" is either (1) to know it as it is *not* in itself, which would be *absolute error*, or else (2) not to know it *at all*, which would be *absolute ignorance*. To one or the other of these all human knowledge is reduced by the common interpretation of the doctrine of the "relativity of knowledge." The world needs a wiser doctrine.

§ 20. So important to a truly scientific theory of the universe is thorough comprehension of the Scientific Theory of Universals, and, in particular, of the principle of the INTELLIGIBLE REALITY OF THE GENUS-IN-ITSELF, that a single clear and simple illustration of this principle will be no waste of space. Let us take the "family" as an easily conceived instance of the real genus in itself.

In modern civilized communities, the political unit is the individual; but the social unit, as distinguished from the political unit, is the family, since society as such consists only of complete and incomplete families. The married individual is a member in each of two complete families — that from which he sprang and that which he himself founds. The unmarried individual is an actual member of the family from which he sprang, and also a possible founder and member of a new family of his own; hence he must be regarded as existing partly in a complete, and partly in an incomplete family.

Every complete family as such is essentially and necessarily composed of several individual members — father, mother, and one or more children. The father is related to the mother as husband, and the mother to the father as wife; their reciprocal relation is marriage. The father and mother are both related to the children as parents, and the children to the father and mother as offspring; their reciprocal relation is parentage, on the one side, and filiation, on the other. The children are related to each other as brothers and sisters: their relation is that of brotherhood or sisterhood. Father, mother, and children, although separate individuals, are constituted a real family by these interrelations of marriage, parentage, filiation, brotherhood, and sisterhood; these family relations themselves, in their totality, make up the family constitution, and are precisely as real as the individuals related, inhering in the family *as such* and *as a whole,* and subsisting neither in any one individual member nor in any outside observer. If there is to be either a real father, a real mother, or a real child, then there must be a real family of all three; there can be no father without a mother and a child, no mother without a father and a child, no child without a father and a mother. Nay, more: no individual as such can exist except as a member of some family precisely as real as himself; the reality of his family is the absolute condition of his own reality, and, *vice versa,* the reality of several individuals is the absolute condition of the reality of the family. All individuals compose the genus family. All families compose the genus society. All societies compose the genus mankind. All individuals = all families = all societies = all mankind.

In this union and interrelation of many in one and one in many, in this immanent relational constitution by which many individuals exist and are indissolubly united in one kind, lies the very essence of the family as such; it is this system of inherent relations, precisely as real as the individuals related, and wholly independent of any outside observer, which constitutes the intelligible and essential reality of the family as a genus in itself. Every family must be relationally constituted in order either *to be* a family or *to be known* as one; every genus must be relationally constituted in order either *to be* a genus or *to be known* as one. Immanent in the very nature of being, this principle of the objectivity or reality of generic relations is the absolute condition of the possibility of a WORLD-ORDER; and, immanent in the very nature of knowledge, it is no less the absolute condition of the possibility of a WORLD-SCIENCE.

§ 21. Now in order to escape from the dense fog of error which, generated by the doctrine of the exclusive subjectivity of relations, has settled heavily down over so-called modern philosophy under the malign influence of the German Theory of Universals, let us imagine an outside observer, as knowing subject, set in actual relation to a particular family, as object known.

I. First of all, it is to be noted that the observer and the family are, numerically considered, *two distinct and independent realities.* So far as they are now related in the mere act of knowledge, one is the subject and the other is the object of this act; to this extent they are reciprocally dependent, — that is, the present act of knowledge is conditioned upon their being brought into present relationship. But, so far as they exist in themselves, neither subject nor object is at all dependent upon the other; the observer is *intelligent in himself*, independently of the family, and the family is *intelligible in itself*, independently of the observer. The present relationship of knowledge is necessary neither to the intelligence of the subject nor to the intelligibility of the object, nor yet to the real existence of either.

II. Next, it is to be noted that *what the subject knows of the object*, in the present relationship, is identical with the *concept which results from that relationship*. If the observer's knowledge is real (that is, if it is neither error nor ignorance mistaken for knowledge), then his concept of the family reproduces subjectively and accurately the objective relational constitution of the family. What the observer knows is, not his own concept, but the family itself; the concept is simply his knowledge of it. Otherwise, the family would not be the object at all — which it must be in the case supposed. As self-conscious, the observer doubtless knows his own knowledge, too; but his knowledge of the family, if real, is primarily knowledge of the family itself, and only secondarily of the concept of the family.

III. Further, it is to be noted that the degree, quantity, and quality of the observer's knowledge of the family, in the case supposed, depend on *two conditions:* (1) on the fulness and accuracy of his previous knowledge of the real genus "family" in general, and (2) on the fulness and accuracy of his observation of this family in particular. If the observer were only a child, he would know little of the real family constitution in general, and would necessarily form a very vague and inadequate concept of this particular family; and so, likewise, if he were a chance visitor from some planet where babies grow on trees or fall in raindrops. Only he who already possesses profound knowledge of a real kind will quickly and thoroughly comprehend a new case of that kind, and then only if he keenly and comprehensively observes it. The adequacy of a concept to its object must always depend on previous thorough understanding of the genus to which the object belongs, and of the lower and higher genera to which this genus is related in Nature. Our observer can "know" the family, as object, on no other terms than these. The price of all knowledge is *experience*, and this price he must pay.

IV. Lastly, it is to be noted that the concept (that is, the observer's actual knowledge of the family) is a *product of two equally real co-factors*, the observer and the family as subject and object. The observer is intelligent in himself,— more or less so according to his native capacity and the amount of his previously acquired knowledge; the family is intelligible in itself,— its intelligibility (since all relations as such are essentially intelligible) being simply the necessary consequence of its relational constitution. The concept, as actual present knowledge of the family by the observer, *results* from bringing an intelligent subject into actual relationship with an intelligible object; it is determined to be what it is, and not otherwise, by the united determinant influences of both. Certainly, if the object did not impress, affect, or act upon the subject in some way or other, it could never be known by the subject at all, and the concept would not in the least degree reproduce its relational constitution — which the concept incontrovertibly does, if it is real knowledge of the object at all. *How* this result comes to pass is a difficult problem, to be solved, if possible, by the Theory of Knowledge; but *that* it comes to pass is an undeniable fact, if any real knowledge exists at all. Whatever theory may be advanced to explain the "origin of knowledge," every such theory must recognize the truth that subject and object are equally real co-factors in all real knowledge, or else must come under the ban of all theories which despise and falsify facts. The influence of the object is proved by the fact that real knowledge of it exists; the influence of the subject is proved by the fact that this real knowledge is limited and imperfect. But the very limitation of real knowledge of the object in itself is proof that such real knowledge exists; for nothing can be limited that is not itself real.

§ 22. Now let us inquire how the observer, as subject, and the family, as object, would be related, if the German Conceptualist Theory of Universals (namely, that the subjective universal concept, or "Vorstellung," and not the objective universal genus, is the real object of knowledge) were true.

It follows from the German Theory that, like husband and wife in the old common law, *the observer and the family are one, and the observer is that one.* According to this theory, the concept is the only real object of knowledge; the genus cannot be admitted to have any reality at all, as distinguished from the concept. But the concept of the family, in the case supposed, exists nowhere but in the observer's mind; hence the family, so far as it really exists, exists only in the observer's mind, and cannot exist at all outside of the observer himself.

The only apparent or plausible escape from this absurd conclusion is to argue that the family at least exists in the concepts of many observers, and therefore must exist outside of any particular observer. But to this argument the reply is obvious and crushing: namely, that "many observers," if thus unguardedly and most naively conceded to exist, would necessarily constitute a real objective genus, independent of our particular observer and all his concepts; and that, if one such real genus may exist and be known as separate from his concept of it, it is preposterously illogical to refuse to recognize another such genus in the family. The German Theory of Universals has but one logical terminus — SOLIPSISM, or the philosophy which denies all real existence except to the solitary philosopher himself.

In short, the German Theory, if logically adhered to,

altogether absorbs or extinguishes the object in the subject, the family in the observer, the universe in the theorist, and destroys thereby the possibility of *any real or scientific knowledge;* while, if not logically adhered to, it is totally worthless for science and philosophy alike. Further criticism of it is unnecessary here. The Scientific Theory of Universals, applied in practice, is the SCIENTIFIC METHOD; and that will be the subject of our next paper.

V.

§ 23. WHAT is the SCIENTIFIC METHOD? Nothing is more common or more confusing than a loose, vague, and indeterminate use of this phrase. It is the object of the present paper to give definiteness and scientific precision to a much abused expression, by showing that the Scientific Method is neither more nor less than the UNIVERSAL LEARNING-PROCESS — the process by which man, individual or collective, has learned everything which he now knows; and, further, by showing that this universal learning-process is neither more nor less than the SCIENTIFIC THEORY OF UNIVERSALS APPLIED IN PRACTICE TO THE ACQUISITION OF KNOWLEDGE.

§ 24. If science is real knowledge of the universe, — that is, neither ignorance nor error mistaken for knowledge, — then, self-evidently, the "method" of science is nothing but the *way* in which that knowledge has been acquired. It is no mystery; it is the familiar process by which we have learned whatever we really know. Common-sense applies this process clumsily on a small scale; the separate sciences apply it skilfully on a large scale, but in arbitrarily limited fields of investigation; philosophy, or WORLD-SCIENCE, applies it skilfully on the largest scale to the universe as a whole. The fundamental identity of the learning-process in common-sense, in science, and in philosophy, — in other words, the absolute *unity and continuity of method in all acquisition of knowledge,* — is the constitutive and distinctive principle of scientific philosophy as such.

Nothing could be more unscientific, unphilosophic, or disastrous to the cause of ripe reason, than the contempt for so-called "common thinking" which is fostered by the unmodernized philosophy grounded on the German Theory of Universals. Common thinking is only immature and inaccurate thinking; but the maturest and most accurate thinking must first pass through the stage of immaturity and inaccuracy. The difference is one of degree only, not of kind. There is but *one universe*, whose particular phenomena change, but whose essential laws are unchanging; there is but *one human reason*, whose special applications vary, but whose essential laws are unvarying; the fundamental unity of the universe and the fundamental unity of human reason logically necessitate a fundamental unity of method in the application of human reason to the universe. Hence it is a thoroughly irrational and incredible supposition that there should be any philosophic method whatever which is fundamentally different from the Scientific Method. The absolute unity and continuity of method in all acquisition of real knowledge is, we repeat, the first principle of a genuinely scientific philosophy.

§ 25. Consider once more, in the light of all that has preceded, how the Scientific Theory of Universals determines necessarily the OBJECT OF KNOWLEDGE, and then note how this determination of the object of knowledge explains the one and only possible way of acquiring knowledge — the universal learning-process or Scientific Method.

I. As already shown at length, the complete object of knowledge is never the *Individual Thing*, never the *Universal Concept*, but always the *Universal Genus*. The Genus is the unity of many individual things reciprocally related in one universal kind; and the intelligible essence of the Genus is this internal relational system of the whole as a whole. The Genus may or may not be related, as a present object of knowledge, to a present subject of knowledge, in a present act of knowledge; but this non-essential and transient relation to a subject in no wise affects or changes the internal self-relatedness in which the intelligible essence of the Genus consists. Nothing but this internal and permanent relational constitution of the Genus-in-itself can explain the fact that, whenever it becomes an object of knowledge, many independent minds or subjects of knowledge derive essentially one and the same concept from it. This significant and pregnant fact did not escape the eagle eye of Kant himself, when he said (Prolegomena, § 18): "There would be no reason why the judgments of other minds should necessarily agree with my own judgments, were it not that the unity of the object to which these judgments all refer, and with which they all agree, requires them all to agree one with another." If Kant had only adhered to this profound insight into the independent, immanent, and determinant constitution of the object as a *known thing-in-itself*, and if he had not constantly neutralized it by declaring the *thing-in-itself unknowable*, the German Theory of Universals would not have been for a hundred years the chief obstacle to the progress of philosophy.

II. The Concept is not an intermediate third term between the object and the subject of knowledge, but is itself the very act or relation of knowledge between them. *The knowing an object is itself the concept of it.* Even a false concept is only partially false — the false combination of elements separately true. Nothing could have been more unfortunate for philosophy than the clumsy "hypostasis," or transformation of a mere act or relation into a thing, by which the Concept has been set up in German metaphysic as itself the only real object of knowledge. The permanence of conceptual knowledge is a fact due to memory; but this fact does not wipe out the other facts that *the object of all knowledge is the genus known*, and that *knowledge perishes when the genus is forgotten*.

III. To the question, "What is that?" the invariable answer is, "A book," "A house," "A tree," or some other kind of things — a genus always. The amount of information imparted by the answer is measured by the amount of knowledge respecting that kind of things already possessed by the inquirer. Nothing whatever is or can be known as absolutely single or unrelated, that is, as out of its kind. The only possible answer to the question, "What is that thing?" is to tell the kind to which that thing belongs. Know the kind, and the thing is so far known; know all the kinds to which it belongs, and the thing would be absolutely or exhaustively known. If absolute or exhaustive knowledge of anything is unattainable by man, the reason is that his knowledge of the innumerable kinds of things is necessarily incomplete. But it is much to know in what knowledge consists — much to know that knowledge is always of the thing through its kind and the kind through its things: in a word, that its object is necessarily and invariably the Genus-in-itself. For it is the fact of the independent, permanent, and immanent self-relatedness of the Genus-in-itself which renders the universe intelligible; and it is thorough understanding and appreciation of this fact which render a philosophy of the universe possible, nay, inevitable. Science has already accumulated abundant materials for a comprehensive world-conception: nothing is now needed but ability to comprehend them.

§ 26. From all this it follows that the learning-process, identical in common-sense, science, and philosophy, must be the patient and continuous DISCOVERY OF GENERA BY EXPERIENCE. If the internal self-relatedness of the Genus exists independently of human reason, yet is knowable and discoverable by it, then the only possible learning-process must be the OBSERVATION OF NATURE. Such has been from the beginning the Scientific Method; and this is nothing but reducing to practice the Scientific Theory of Universals, namely, that the real object of knowledge is the Genus alone. As so often happens, practice has gone in advance of theory; yet theory alone ultimately explains practice. Scientific practice took for granted the existence and knowableness of genera and species, and their discoverability by observation. Indifferent to all philosophical skepticism, it resolutely set to work to discover them; and the result has been such a vast accumulation of indubitable knowledge of Nature as to confound and overawe skepticism itself. In making the initial assumption of knowable and discoverable genera in Nature, and in employing observation and experiment as its means of investigation, science has only improved upon the immemorial method of common-sense — the method which every child necessarily adopts in its earliest acquisition of knowledge, the method which every man adopts in the world of affairs, the method which every skeptic himself adopts in his ordinary life. And it turns out in the end that this practical method, tested by a thoroughly modernized theory of universals, is at bottom the only philosophical method — the only possible foundation of a scientific philosophy.

For from the German Theory of Universals, that the real object of knowledge is the Concept alone, it follows that the whole learning-process consists in the mere DISCOVERY OF CONCEPTS BY CONSCIOUSNESS and the DEVELOPMENT OF CONCEPTS BY PURE REASON, independently of real genera and species in Nature as a known thing-in-itself. Hence Kant unequivocally declares (Prolegomena, § 36): "The [human] understanding does not derive its own *a priori* laws from Nature, but prescribes them to it." Again (§ 38): "The unity of objects is determined merely by the [human] understanding, and indeed according to conditions which lie in its own constitution; and thus the [human] understanding is the origin of the universal order of Nature, since it comprehends all phenomena under its own laws," *etc.* In other words, Nature, as a reality existing independently of the human understanding, has no discoverable unity or order whatever, and is absolutely unknowable in itself. This is a flat denial of the results of science, which consist in verified discoveries of an *immanent and generic* order and unity of Nature, known by, but in itself independent of, the human understanding. Thus the German Theory of Universals, denying all knowledge of real genera in themselves, denies the truth of science, and the possibility of any method by which the immanent constitution of Nature may be learned by man; and there we leave it.

§ 27. Now the Scientific Method, whether practised unskilfully and narrowly by common-sense, skilfully and broadly by science, or profoundly and comprehensively by philosophy, consists in three essential steps.

I. OBSERVATION. Man *observes* Nature, and thereby gradually discovers its real genera. Since the real object of knowledge is invariably the Genus-in-itself, there must be observation and comparison of many individual things before the generic relations which unite them in one natural kind can be even in part discovered, — that is, before knowledge as such begins. These generic relations ramify far beyond the reach of exhaustive observation by man. Hence result the actual limitation and imperfection of human knowledge, on the one hand, and, on the other hand, the absurdity of setting up any arbitrary or fixed limits of human knowledge, so long as there is a possibility of making further observation, or of inventing artificial aids to observation, or of strengthening and developing the observing powers themselves. Grant the existence of observing powers in Man and the existence of genera to be observed in Nature, and science is possible; deny either factor of human knowledge, and science is impossible. It is wholly immaterial to the truth of science whether we can, or cannot, frame a Theory of Knowledge which shall explain exactly and fully in what observation itself consists. *How* we observe may be doubtful; *that* we observe is indubitable. Kant reasons that we have no faculty by which to observe things in themselves, and therefore cannot know them; scientific philosophy reasons that we do know genera in themselves, and therefore must have faculties by which to observe them. The very first step in learning anything is Observation, and common-sense, science, and philosophy alike would be impossible without it.

II. HYPOTHESIS. Man not only observes real genera in being, but also creates ideal generalizations in thought. By imagination, inference, and reasoning, he combines the data of observation into tentative concepts of possible real kinds. All reasoning is classification. Deduction is reasoning from the constitution of the universal kind to that of its individual things; induction is reasoning from the constitution of the individual things to that of their universal kind. The syllogism itself, the universal type and instrument of all reasoning, affirms both in premises and in conclusion the reality of generic relations, and absolutely presupposes the truth of the Scientific Theory of Universals. Hypothesis, the only means by which man can freely enlarge his intellectual horizon, is itself a mere bridge between initial observation and final observation. For no hypothesis as such is knowledge; but hypothesis becomes knowledge, when new experience has set upon it the seal of its own confirmation.

III. EXPERIMENTAL VERIFICATION. This is the testing of hypothesis by fresh observation. If an ideal generalization, subjected to this crucial test, proves to have been a genuine anticipation of experience, it can only be because fresh observation at last finds the real genus which the ideal generalization anticipated, and to the discovery of which it successfully guided. This is the essence of all Verification, the last step of the Scientific Method, the confirmation of hypothesis by fresh observation, the discovery in Nature of a real genus which an ideal generalization sagaciously divined in thought. The Scientific Method begins with OBSERVATION, proceeds with HYPOTHESIS, and ends with FRESH OBSERVATION IN EXPERIMENTAL VERIFICATION; and what it observes, what it anticipates, what it verifies,— in one word, what it learns, — is invariably the REAL GENUS-IN-ITSELF.

§ 28. Thus the Scientific Method, or the universal learning-process by which all human knowledge is acquired, is neither more nor less than the Scientific Theory of Universals reduced to practice. The doctrine of the REAL GENUS-IN-ITSELF, as discovered by the Scientific Method, is the THEORY OF BEING; and that will be the subject of our next paper.

VI.

§ 29. The Scientific, Modern, or American Theory of Universals, which results necessarily from analysis of the Scientific Method, is SCIENTIFIC REALISM, as opposed to PHILOSOPHICAL IDEALISM; and it determines the subdivision of scientific philosophy into its three great departments, the theories of BEING, of KNOWING, and of DOING. The Scientific Theory of Being results from analysis of the GENUS-IN-ITSELF, and constitutes Ontology or CONSTRUCTIVE REALISM, as opposed to all forms of Constructive Idealism. The Scientific Theory of Knowledge results from analysis of the CONCEPT, and constitutes Psychology or CRITICAL REALISM, as opposed to all forms of Transcendental or Critical Idealism. The Scientific Theory of Conduct results from analysis of the WORD, and constitutes Anthroponomy (including Ethics, Politics, and Art in its widest sense), Sociology, or ETHICAL REALISM, as opposed to all forms of Ethical Idealism. The Scientific Theory of the Universe, as the absolute union of Being, Knowing, and Doing in the One and All, results from comprehension of these three theories in complete organic unity, and constitutes Organic Philosophy, Scientific Theology, or RELIGIOUS REALISM, as opposed to all forms of Religious Idealism.

§ 30. The problem of the scientific theory of Being is to determine, so far as it can be determined by the philosophical use of the scientific method, the actual constitution of the universe as a whole, that is, as the *Highest Known Kind of Real or Concrete Being;* and thereby to form a SCIENTIFIC WORLD-CONCEPTION.

§ 31. In order to grasp the full meaning of this problem, let us take, for example, a familiar instance of the known kind in the human race. The words "Man," "Humanity," and "Mankind," although in popular use employed vaguely and almost interchangeably, will serve our turn, if for present purposes we may be permitted to limit their signification by precise definitions.

By "Man," then, let us understand the CONCRETE INDIVIDUAL; that is, any and every living member of the human race in the fulness of his individual reality, including, on the one hand, all that is peculiar to him as a particular man, and, on the other hand, all that is common to him with other men in general.

By "Humanity," let us understand the ABSTRACT CLASS ESSENCE, including only the universal nature which is common to all men as a class, and excluding all that is peculiar to each particular man as an individual. "Humanity" thus expresses what we all know as "human nature," which everybody recognizes as a mere abstraction by itself alone, and which nobody nowadays mistakes for an independent reality; it is real, but real only as existing in all real men.

Lastly, by "Mankind," let us understand the CONCRETE UNIVERSAL KIND OR GENUS, the human race as a whole, including all concrete individuals with all their individual peculiarities, and including, therefore, that universal "human nature" which, though a mere abstraction by itself alone, is nevertheless completely realized in each real individual, and in the race as a real whole of real individuals.

§ 32. These definitions bring out clearly the fact that "Humanity," the abstract class essence, is realized equally in the individual, "Man," and in the genus, "Mankind"; it constitutes that by which we reason from one to the other. Such is necessarily the case with every genus. In every genus, the constitution of the CONCRETE INDIVIDUAL and the constitution of the CONCRETE KIND reciprocally make known or reveal each other, just so far as each realizes and contains the ABSTRACT CLASS ESSENCE. True, the individual has his individual peculiarities, such as his "face" or "make" of individual features as a whole, which is never exactly duplicated in any other individual; while the genus equally has its generic peculiarities, such as heredity, bisexuality, gregariousness, and all other attributes which can exist only through the social correlation of many individuals in one kind. These peculiarities are not common both to genus and to individual; but the abstract class essence, unreal by itself alone, yet realized in both, is common to both. Hence the constitutions of the genus as genus and of the individual as individual, containing equally this common identical element, necessarily repeat, reflect, or reveal each other to that extent; knowledge of this common element in one is necessarily knowledge of it in the other also. The individual is a known fact; society is no less a known fact; but each is known only through the other, and what makes either known is what makes both known at the same time. This is the reason why, in general, the individual thing can be known only through its kind, and the kind only through its individual things. Upon this great principle of the RECIPROCAL REVELATION OF THING AND KIND rests, on the one hand, the possibility of *Induction*, or reasoning from the constitution of individual things to that of their universal kind, and, on the other hand, the possibility of *Deduction*, or reasoning from the constitution of a universal kind to that of its individual things. It is the antecedent condition, not only of all scientific hypothesis, but even of the syllogism itself, the universal type and instrument of all reasoning whatever. It is safe to say, therefore, that no principle, whether in formal or in applied logic, has a firmer foundation in science, nay, in the eternal constitution of reason itself, than this principle which results from analysis of the Real Genus-in-itself: namely, THE INDIVIDUAL CONCRETE THING AND THE UNIVERSAL CONCRETE KIND REVEAL EACH OTHER THROUGH

THE ABSTRACT CLASS ESSENCE WHICH IS COMMON TO BOTH. On its logical side, this principle is the *Fundamental Law of Human Knowledge;* on its ontological side, it is the *Fundamental Law of the Natural Self-Revelation of Being to Thought.* It constitutes, therefore, the foundation of the Scientific Theory of Being.

§ 33. Now it is precisely this profound and irrefutable principle, this indispensable basis of all science and all reasoning, this necessary constitution of the Real Genus which renders the universe intelligible by mind, that Agnosticism unwittingly and blunderingly violates. Philosophical, conceptualistic, or idealistic Agnosticism builds in vain on the exploded German Theory of Universals (see §§ 9– 22), and needs no further notice here. Popular Agnosticism, however, which has no Theory of Universals and therefore no Philosophy at all, professes to build on the facts of science, and to be as realistic as science itself. While it claims scientific knowledge of genera and species in Nature, as real kinds of real things, it at the same time denies all scientific knowledge of Nature in its infinite unity, as the supreme Kind of Kinds,—denies, that is, the possibility of a SCIENTIFIC WORLD-CONCEPTION. It thus proves itself totally incapable of perceiving that, from the mere logical nature of the case, *scientific knowledge of finite genera-in-themselves is necessarily, just so far, scientific knowledge of the Infinite Genus-in-itself*—totally incapable of perceiving that *two* in one hand and *two* in the other hand constitute *four* in both hands. In other words, popular Agnosticism possesses all the elements of a Scientific World-Conception, but does not possess synthetic ability enough to put them together or see the whole in the sum of the parts.

For, precisely as the individual thing is related to its kind, so is the kind related to its superior kind, this to the kind next superior, and so on till that highest kind of all is reached which is identical with Nature, the Universe, the One and All of Existence,— with Infinite Real Being; and, precisely as the constitution of the lowest kind is manifested or revealed in the constitution of the lowest individual thing of that kind through the abstract class essence which is common to both, so is the constitution of the supreme Kind of Kinds, or Infinite Real Being, manifested or revealed in the constitution of the whole vast chain of kinds down to that *individuum* which closes the series, be it atom, ether-unit, monad-soul, or what it may. The minimum of real knowledge, therefore, is, *just so far*, real knowledge of the constitution of the Universe in its unity, totality, and infinitude. In other words, the nature of the Infinite Whole reveals itself necessarily in the nature of each and all of its infinitesimal parts and each and all of its included kinds, in proportion to the relative elevation of each part or kind in the scale of being. This not only is so, but must be so, if the Scientific Theory of Universals is true; and there is no truth in science or in human reason, if that theory is false. It is logically impossible to deny all scientific knowledge of the Universe in its infinite unity without at the same time denying all scientific knowledge of it in its infinite multiplicity; for knowledge of the least of its parts is, precisely to that extent, knowledge of the whole. If popular Agnosticism only had enough philosophy to understand and follow out the logic of its own denials, it would be a mad plunge into bottomless, shoreless, skyless Ignorance — the suicide of reason itself in a delirium of cowardice and self-distrust. From this self-annihilation it escapes only by contradicting itself more stoutly and more unblushingly than the Athanasian Creed; and for this reason alone it is safe to predict that the reign of the Agnostic Creed over modern liberalism will be short.

§ 34. In its simplest form, then, the problem of the Scientific Theory of Being is: " *What kind of a Universe is this?*" Either the Universe is of no kind at all (which is absurd), or else its kind must be determined and discovered in strict accordance with the known universal law of all kinds: namely, the *Reciprocal Revelation of Thing and Kind through the Abstract Class Essence which is common to both.* The problem can be solved only on the principle that the essential constitution of the Universe more or less repeats, reflects and reveals itself in miniature in the constitution of each of the innumerable concrete kinds of which it is itself the absolute unity, although it cannot completely reveal itself except to itself in this same absolute unity. It is not necessary that all of these kinds contained within the Universe should be known by man, in order to enable him to attain real knowledge of the constitution of the Universe as a whole, and thereby to form a scientific world-conception; real knowledge of any of these kinds is, just so far, real knowledge of the Universe as the supreme Kind of Kinds, and, the better its internal subordinate kinds are known, so much the greater will be man's knowledge of the supreme Kind of Kinds itself. Hence the orderly progress of science is the natural growth of man's knowledge of Infinite Being, and constitutes REVELATION in that strictly natural sense of the word in which alone science can employ it.

Anything arbitrary, miraculous, or supernatural, anything beyond or contrary to experience, anything inconsistent with known fact or known law, anything incapable of verification by ascertained congruity with the already ascertained Order of Nature, would be utterly inadmissible in scientific philosophy, and therefore utterly inadmissible here. For this reason the thoroughly transcendental conception of the "Unknowable," in any other sense than that of the *Non-Existent* or the *Nonsensical*, must be rigorously excluded as a mere superstition, since it confessedly denotes that which is beyond all possible knowledge or experience.

The Unknown, however, must be admitted to be as certainly real as the Known, since every step in the triumphant march of science, every discovery in the long history of man, has essentially consisted in the conversion of the Unknown into the Known, and since thus, by the widest possible induction, the reality of the Unknown has been established beyond all controversy as an object of perpetually possible experience. No "transcendental" conception — no conception, that is, which transcends actual or possible experience — can be recognized as legitimate in scientific philosophy; there is no such thing, therefore, as "Transcendental Realism" — a name which is self-contradictory, and hence utterly devoid of meaning.

It remains now to apply the principle of the *Reciprocal Revelation of Thing and Kind* to the solution of the problem of the Scientific Theory of Being: "What kind of a Universe is this?"

§ 35. The Universe, as the supreme Kind of Kinds which contains all other kinds within itself, is the real genus-in-itself in its absolute and all-comprehensive mode of INFINITE BEING. It cannot, therefore, exist as one among many universes of like nature; it must be the One and All, or it is not the universe. Hence the multiplicity involved in the essence of every kind as such must be found, in the case of the supreme Kind of Kinds, not outside of, but within, its own infinite unity; that is, the constitution of the Universe as a whole cannot be discovered by comparing it with other infinite wholes (but one infinite whole being possible), but only by studying the constitution of its own finite parts. Each known part reveals one real character of the whole; all the known parts together reveal all the real characters of the whole which have thus far come within the reach of human knowledge. Whatever parts or characters remain still unknown can only supplement, never subvert, the reality of those already known.

Otherwise knowledge itself is an absolute impossibility, science is all an illusion, and, as Pindar sang, "Man is a shadow's dream."

§ 36. Now each of the real and concrete forms of existence which are known to man, boundless as their number and variety may appear, falls nevertheless under one or another of three great categorical TYPES OF REAL BEING: namely, the MACHINE, the ORGANISM, and the PERSON. The grounds of this division cannot be given at present; they will sufficiently manifest themselves in the course of what follows. The original question, "What kind of a Universe is this?" becomes now the more definite question, "To which of the three great types of real being, Machine, Organism, or Person, does the Universe belong?" The subject of our next paper will be to consider whether the Machine alone constitutes an adequate basis for a scientific world-conception.

VII.

§ 37. The real essence of the individual thing and the real essence of the universal kind more or less repeat, exemplify, and manifest each other through the abstract class essence which is common to both. This fundamental law of the RECIPROCAL REVELATION OF THING AND KIND (see §§ 31, 32) is inherent in the constitution of every real genus-in-itself; it is equally inherent in the constitution of every concept. Hence it constitutes, on the one hand, the LAW OF THE NATURAL SELF-REVELATION OF BEING TO THOUGHT, and, on the other hand, the ABSOLUTE CONDITION OF HUMAN KNOWLEDGE; and the scientific method is the practical application of it in the study of Nature. The abstract class essence of a kind, determined exactly (though never exhaustively) by the scientific method, is identical, as a system of relations, with the SCIENTIFIC CONCEPT of that kind, and, by means of scientific nomenclature, receives measurably exact verbal embodiment in the SCIENTIFIC DEFINITION. Upon the possibility of this exact determination and discrimination of real kinds in the real system of Nature, giving rise to a complete hierarchy of scientific concepts of abstract class essences, depends unconditionally the possibility of all SCIENTIFIC CLASSIFICATION. Science would vanish into Nescience, if these principles of Scientific Realism could be overthrown.

§ 38. Now the great system of natural classification, carried as far as possible by the various special sciences in their various limited fields of investigation, must be carried still further by scientific philosophy or World-Science, and culminates in the discovery of THREE PRIMORDIAL TYPES OF REAL BEING IN NATURE, so far as Nature has yet come within the scope of the investigating faculties of mankind. The physical sciences find their ultimate concrete unit in the Atom, as individualized out of universal cosmical Ether, — the physiological or biological sciences in the Cell, as individualized out of universal living Protoplasm, — and the psychological or moral sciences in the Self, as individualized out of universal human Mind; but they find their proximate concrete units respectively in the Machine, the Organism, and the Person. It is upon these three Natural Types of Real Being, as actually known in human experience, that scientific philosophy must found its only possible scientific world-conception or Idea of Nature.

§ 39. Let us, then, begin by determining exactly the scientific concept of the Machine, as we find it actually and concretely presented in human experience, in order to discover how far it throws light upon the total constitution of Nature; that is, how far it is scientifically legitimate, in accordance with the law of the reciprocal revelation of thing and kind, to conceive the Universe in its unity as a Machine.

§ 40. Professor T. M. Goodeve (*The Elements of Mechanism*, London, 1886), begins his treatise with the following definition: "A Machine is an assemblage of moving parts, constructed for the purpose of transmitting motion or force, and of modifying, in various ways, the motion or force so transmitted."

A distinguished physicist, in a private letter to the writer under date of June 6, 1889, gives another definition, substantially identical with the preceding, but in some respects more precise from an exclusively mechanical point of view: "My definition of a Machine is a collocation of matter having for its function the transference of motion or the transformation of motion."

It will be noticed by keen critics that, in these definitions, (1) the Machine is only vaguely conceived as a unit, and (2) that the expressions "constructed for the purpose" and "having for its function" both introduce extra-mechanical conceptions — the former a conception which is strictly psychological, and the latter a conception which is strictly physiological (not here mathematical). It is possible to devise a rigorously mechanical definition, as follows: —

A Machine is a material Whole of collocated material Parts, by which, both as Whole and as Parts, Motion is either transferred or transformed.

§ 41. For all the uses of mechanics or physics, this last definition is quite sufficient, because these sciences very properly limit their consideration of the Machine to its exclusively physical and mathematical relations, which have nothing to do with the questions, "Who made it?" and "What was it made for?" They are satisfied, therefore, with an extremely imperfect and mutilated concept of the Machine; their special problems never involve that concept in its fulness and integrity, as it is derived from all actual experience. The anthropological sciences, however, such as sociology, archæology, or political economy, could not advance a step, if they were limited to that skeleton concept of a purely ABSTRACT MACHINE, transcending all actual and possible experience, which satisfies all the requirements of physics or mechanics; it is the REAL MACHINE, not the ghost of it, — or rather the full and integral concept of the Real Machine as drawn from human experience, not this same concept with essential parts omitted, — which alone can satisfy the requirements of the anthropological sciences. Hence we find two widely different concepts of the Machine, one lopped or truncated in physics and mechanics, the other rounded and complete in anthropology, yet both equally scientific and equally useful as the basis of sound scientific inferences.

§ 42. For instance, take the axe — a tool being only a very simple case of the Machine.

Physics would consider the axe in use (an axe not in use

would cease to be a Machine at all) as being only a mass of matter in motion, and doing work in the communication of motion to some other mass of matter — would calculate its momentum, or quantity of motion, as the product of its mass by its velocity, and its striking force, or kinetic energy, as the product of half its mass by the square of its velocity. That is, physics would conceive the axe *solely as a link in the great chain of physical causes and effects* — would recognize it only as under the law of causality, and ignore it altogether as under the law of finality — would treat it exclusively as a material fact, and refuse all inquiry into its origin or purposes as involving extra-physical conceptions and problems. And this eviscerated concept of the Abstract Machine, being sufficient for all purely physical problems, would be all that is properly admissible into the science of pure physics.

But anthropology would consider the axe only as a Real Machine — would conceive it as essentially a tool or weapon constructed by man, and constituted as a causal means to some definite human end, such as chopping wood or killing an enemy. This is the concept of the axe in its essence and its integrity, as a Real Machine known in human experience. If a stone axe-head were found buried deeply in some ancient alluvial deposit, archæology would take it to be a cogent proof of the existence of man himself as its maker in immemorial antiquity, and would reconstruct out of it a whole past of palæolithic or neolithic savagery. This inference of archæology would be precisely as sound, scientific, and necessary as any possible inference of physics, and would lead to this general anthropological definition: —

A Machine is a Causal Means between Man and some definite Human End, both external to the Machine itself.

Is it not plain that, in order to understand the Real Machine in its integrity, as opposed to the Abstract Machine in its partiality, science itself requires us to supplement the physical with the anthropological concept of it, at least so far as to recognize the causal and the teleological elements as equally essential in its constitution?

§ 43. Scientific philosophy, however, must see further than physics, anthropology, or any other special science. Franklin described man as "the tool-making animal"; and the construction of machinery in general unquestionably lies at the foundation of all civilization. From the simple tool, such as the axe, the needle, or the fork, up to the vastest and most complicated machine, such as the printing-press, the Jacquard silk-loom, the ship, the factory, the cathedral, the railroad, the telegraph, or the city, the construction of machinery, as the practical work of intelligence in the subjection of external Nature to man, is, in one point of view, at once the cause and the effect of all human progress in the knowledge of Nature; for, in telescope, microscope, spectroscope, laboratory, observatory, museum, or library, science, no less than industry and commerce, depends upon the Real Machine.

But man is not the only animal which makes machines. Honeycombs, ant-hills, spider-webs, birdsnests, beaver-dams, fox-burrows,— all such constructions are essentially machines; nay, even climbing-plants convert projections or mere roughnesses of contiguous surfaces into ladders or machines for raising themselves into the sunlight. It matters not whether the end which a given machine effects originates in human reason, in animal instinct, or in the depths of organic constitution as such: the essence of the Real Machine is *to mediate causally between an Organism and its End*, and whatever does that is a Real Machine.

§ 44. Let us see, then, whether it may not be possible to comprehend all the elements of truth contained in the physical and the anthropological definitions of the Machine in a higher philosophical definition. It is the aim of physics to include only the strictly causal element in its concept, and carefully to exclude from it all recognition of the teleological element; hence the result is a definition of the Abstract Machine, quite adequate to all the problems of physics, but totally inadequate to problems involving the Real Machine. It is the aim of anthropology to include in its concept both the causal and the teleological elements so far as they relate to man, but no further; hence the result is a definition of the Real Machine, adequate to the problems of anthropology, but inadequate to all higher problems. It is the aim of scientific philosophy, however, to include in its concept ample recognition of both of the equally essential elements, causal and teleological, and, by scrupulously adapting it to all known forms of the Real Machine, to render the concept itself adequate to whatever problems actual human experience may present. Hence we may accept the following as a partial and provisional philosophical definition: —

A Real Machine is a material Whole of collocated material Parts, constructed by an Organism as a Causal Means to some definite Organic End of its own, and so constituted throughout as to effect this End by either transferring or transforming Motion.

§ 45. This concept of the Machine, as is self-evident, contains all the essential elements of the physical and the anthropological concepts, but is more comprehensive than either. It recognizes fully the physical or causal element, and thereby completely includes the Abstract Machine of physics; it recognizes fully the teleological element, and thereby converts the Abstract Machine of physics into the Real Machine of anthropology; it universalizes the Real Machine of anthropology so as to relate it to the whole organic kingdom, shows that the concepts of the Machine and of the Organism are universally, necessarily, and inseparably connected, and thereby raises both concepts to the level of scientific philosophy.

But still something is wanting to a complete comprehension of the Real Machine. What is the nature of this universal, necessary, and inseparable connection between the Machine and the Organism? Pressing onward to find an answer to this question, we are led to a discovery of supreme importance: namely, that *the constitutions of the Machine and of the Organism involve each the other, and therefore are intelligible each through the other alone.*

§ 46. In the light of this principle, the Real Machine appears in a strikingly new aspect. When it is said in common speech, "The man cuts the grass," "The man shoots the bird," or "The man writes the letter," the expression is not literally true; for it is the scythe that cuts, the gun that shoots, the pen that writes. But there is a profound truth in the common phrases. For the man and the scythe, the man and the gun, the man and the pen, constitute together, in each case, a larger organic whole; and it is really this larger organic whole, this SELF-EXTENDED ORGANISM, which does the act. The scythe, the gun, and the pen are, in truth, only so many artificial prolongations and special modifications of the *hand;* and by these, as causal means, the man himself is enabled to perform acts otherwise impossible. That is to say, the scythe, the gun, or the pen,—in general, the Real Machine,—is only an ARTIFICIAL AND SEPARABLE ORGAN FOR SELF-EXTENSION OF THE ORGANISM. When not used, it is only a functionless lump of matter; when used, it derives from the Organism a transient and artificial life as a temporary Organ; its only life lies in its use, and lasts only so long as it is used.

§ 47. Still more striking, in the light of the same principle, is the new aspect in which the Organism itself appears. Every single organ in the Organism appears in a new aspect as itself a NATURAL MACHINE, since it invariably functions as a causal means between the entire Organism and some definite Organic End. But, instead of originating in any constructive process of which the Organism as a whole is conscious, the single organ originates in that unconscious process of self-evolution by which the Organism as a whole comes into being through the inwardly constructive forces of Nature. Hence the Organism itself, as a unitary complex of organs which mediates causally between itself and all its own Organic Ends, necessarily appears in a new aspect as, in truth, a SELF-MAKING AND SELF-WORKING NATURAL MACHINE.

§ 48. Thus we find ourselves led irresistibly, by a chain of conclusive scientific reasoning, to this complete and final philosophical definition of the Real Machine: —

A Real Machine is a material Whole of collocated material Parts, constructed by an Organism as a Causal Means to some definite Organic End of its own, and so constituted throughout as to effect this End by either transferring or transforming Motion. Every Real Machine is either artificial or natural, the Artificial Real Machine being an Artificial Organ of the Natural Organism, and the Natural Real Machine being the Natural Organism itself; and every Real Organism is a Self-Making and Self-Working Real Machine.

It remains, in our next paper, to consider what will be the result of applying the concept of the Machine, as successively elaborated by physics, by anthropology and by scientific philosophy, to the formation of a Scientific World-Conception or Theory of Being.

VIII.

§ 49. THE science of arithmetic conceives the one and the many as mere relations of quantity in Abstract Number, and disregards altogether the Real Things without which no relations of number can be real. The science of geometry conceives the point, the line, the surface, and the solid as mere relations of quantity in Abstract Form, and disregards altogether the Real Substance without which no relations of form can be real. In general, the sciences of pure mathematics form no concepts except those of Abstract Quantity, Number, and Form, out of which no scientific world-conception could possibly be constructed except that of a purely ABSTRACT UNIVERSE; for they rigorously suppress or exclude all concepts of Real Substance as essentially non-mathematical.

The sciences of chemistry and physics, however, while adopting and using the mathematical concepts of Abstract Quantity, Number, and Form, introduce new concepts of their own in those of Real Matter as Mass or Molecule, Real Motion, and Real Force or Energy. Chemistry deals with the molecular motions and forces of matter, physics with its molar motions and forces; both sciences, however, agree in rejecting from their concepts all recognition of the relation of *End and Means*, and including in them recognition of the relation of physical *Cause and Effect* alone. Hence the physical or chemico-physical concept of Real Substance is that of the ABSTRACT MACHINE alone, not of the REAL MACHINE in its wholeness at all (see §§ 40–48).

These skeleton concepts of mathematics, mechanics, physics, and chemistry are perfectly true as far as they go, and no one can think mathematically or physically except by taking and using them as they are. Not the slightest doubt or slur is here meant to be cast upon the right to employ strictly mathematical concepts alone in mathematics, or strictly physical concepts alone in physics; the progress of science would be rendered difficult, perhaps impossible, without that division of labor which can be effected only by the legitimate use of abstractions. But no possible use of abstractions which separate what is really inseparable can lead to a scientific theory of Real Being as a whole. When it comes to that, scientific concepts drawn from reality in all the fulness and integrity of actual human experience can alone avail to frame a really scientific world-conception, a truly philosophic Idea of Nature; and philosophy, or universal science, is just as much entitled, nay, just as much necessitated as any special science to frame concepts of its own, provided that in framing them it scrupulously follows the scientific method.

§ 50. Now the physical concept of the Abstract Machine, like the mathematical concept of Abstract Quantity, can, if applied to the formation of a world-theory, yield only the concept of an ABSTRACT UNIVERSE; it can never yield more than certain elements, fragmentary and few, of the concept of the REAL UNIVERSE. Refusing as it does all consideration of the relation of End and Means, and recognizing only the relation of Cause and Effect, the science of physics has no principle save the principle of causality upon which it can claim to ground a cosmical theory. It must conceive all events whatever as exclusively physical events, as nothing but motions in masses of matter; and it must explain all sequence in these motions as governed exclusively by physical causation. No other concept than this of a purely Abstract Universe, in which nothing can ever manifest itself except the monotonous reign of iron physical necessity, can possibly be extracted from the Abstract Machine of physics. But let us see whether this abortive concept of universal physical necessity alone can maintain itself under a close and keen scrutiny.

§ 51. If, for instance, all the motions of matter which occur throughout Space at any given instant of Time could be comprehended as one infinitely complex motion, pure physics would conceive this one complex motion as the physical resultant or effect of a similar complex motion in the instant next preceding; and all motions in the history of the cosmos would thus be reduced to a single concatenated series reaching back into a limitless past,— an infinite regress in which each term would be at once an effect to its antecedent and a cause to its consequent. In this case (which is simply an attempt to conceive the Abstract Machine as the Abstract Universe), what rational notion could be formed of the causal nexus itself, as uniting antecedent and consequent? The Abstract Machine is abstracted from the Real Machine, tacitly even by physics; but an Abstract Universe would necessarily be in itself all in all, and there could be, therefore, no Real Universe, more inclusive than itself, from which to abstract it. If physical causality, then, were the sole real principle of the universe, what must be the nature of the causal relation itself?

§ 52. M. Deschanel (*Elementary Treatise on Natural Philosophy*, Everett's revised sixth edition, New York, 1883) defines Force as follows: "Force may be defined as that which *tends to produce* motion in a body at rest, or *to produce* change of motion in a body which is moving. . . We obtain the idea of force *through our own conscious exercise of muscular force*, and we can approximately estimate the amount of a force (if not too great or too small) *by the effort which we have to make* to resist it; as when we try the weight of a body by lifting it."

M. Naville (*Modern Physics*, Downton's translation, Edinburgh, 1884, p. 35) similarly says: "The idea of force has its origin *in the action which we exert* upon our organs, and by our organs upon foreign bodies. If we *take away* [*abstract*] *the sense of an initial and free power*, there remains the idea of a simple motive power. This power, *separated* [*abstracted*] *from its immediate consciousness*, is no longer conceivable than in the manifestation of its effects; and therefore force, as it is considered in physics, has no other determination possible than the motion which it produces.". . . "The doctrine of the inertia of matter is the centre of all the conceptions of modern physics. . . Inertia excludes from matter all power of its own, other than that which relates to the occupation of place and to motion; it therefore reduces the conception of bodies to mechanical elements" (*Ibid.* p. 42). Countless passages of like tenor might be cited. The italics in these passages are ours.

CONSCIOUS EFFORT, then, is the only experiential origin and ground of our concept or rational notion of *Force in Nature*, as efficient cause, effectuating energy, or dynamical antecedent of the consequent "effect"—the *ex-factum*, "that which is out-made (from within the cause itself)." Now this something within the "efficient" or "out-making" cause which is "out-made" in the "effect" is, in every case of conscious effort, a *preconceived end*. We are utterly incapable of making any conscious effort except in order to do something, to accomplish some preconceived end; we, as conscious causes or forces in Nature, necessarily *unite in ourselves both preconceived end and executive energy*, as the absolutely essential elements of every effort; and we know nothing of our own executive energy except as we exercise it in putting forth or executing the preconceived end. In all effort, the two elements of end and energy are indissolubly united. So far as it can be understood through conscious effort, therefore, Force in Nature is the executive energy which puts forth some preconceived end into outward fact: THE REAL CAUSE OUT-MAKES THE PRECONCEIVED END IN THE REAL EFFECT, AND THE REAL EFFECT IS THE

Out-Made Preconceived End of the Real Cause. Hence the two concepts of Efficient Causality and Finality are inextricably interlinked and united in that of Real Conscious Effort, as two inseparable elements of one rational notion; and, since the concept of Motive Force, or Dynamic Cause, is confessedly derived, even in physics, from Real Conscious Effort alone, as its only origin and ground in human experience, *it cannot be formed at all as a rational notion, if either of these inseparable elements is arbitrarily suppressed.*

§ 53. From these results it follows that the concept of an Abstract Universe founded upon that of the Abstract Machine is, if taken absolutely, not only irrational, but impossible; for it destroys itself. As we have just seen, Causality and Finality are intelligible only through each other, and neither by itself alone is intelligible at all; hence an infinite regress of causes and effects from which all relation of ends and means should be rigorously excluded would be rigorously unthinkable, because empty and nonsensical. Looked at externally, such a series would show no causal nexus whatever, no principle of rational connection among the terms; nothing would be observable but mere sequence or time-succession. It is only when looked at from within that a principle of rational connection and unity is discoverable in the *indissoluble union of causality and finality.* In the case of an infinite regress of causes and effects with no ends and means, the only possible experiential concept of Motive Force, Kinetic Energy, or Dynamical Cause would be irretrievably broken up, and would therefore disappear; the relation of cause and effect would itself vanish together with that of end and means; nothing would be left but the relation of antecedent and consequent — mere sequence or time-succession. All communication of motion from body to body would, as Descartes discovered, become essentially incomprehensible. In trying to isolate the *Principle of Motion as Cause and Effect without End and Means*, physics would extinguish Causality by suppressing Finality and Efficiency at once; its own principle of the ABSTRACT CAUSE would slip through its fingers altogether, and it would retain nothing but the principle of SUCCESSION IN TIME. Hence the Abstract Universe of physics would lose all principle of rational unity whatever, and crumble away into the impalpable dust of an infinitude of Atoms, whose motions would manifest no other coherence than that of a mere irrational TIME-SERIES.

§ 54. A sufficient proof of this conclusion is the confirmation of it given by the history of human thought; for, whenever the attempt has been made to conceive the course of Nature causally, but not teleologically, the inevitable result has been, as in the case of Descartes, Hume, Comte, John Stuart Mill, and countless others, to deny efficient causality altogether, and to resolve the causal nexus into the relation of mere invariable antecedence and consequence. But the result of this perfectly logical procedure is a denial of all real unity in Nature: the infinite series of motions in matter becomes a mere time-series, without any rational or comprehensible connection among the terms, and Nature itself breaks up into a chaos of atoms, an infinitude of material units, moving externally according to no discoverable or intelligible law. This is the suicide of all cosmical science, including physics itself. The One is lost irrecoverably in the infinitely Many; and the only possible Theory of Being which remains is that of chaotic and irrational PLURALISM.

§ 55. In fine, physics alone can never become philosophy. The Abstract Machine (the Real Machine from which it is abstracted being tacitly recognized in the background, though not directly employed, by physics itself) is a legitimate scientific concept, indispensable in purely physical problems. But the concept of an Abstract Universe as an

Absolute Unit, *with no recognition whatever of a Real Universe from which to abstract it,*— an Abstract Universe with no unifying principle but that of an Abstract Cause, which, *being just as empty of causal efficiency as it is of causal finality, excludes all real communication of motion,*— this concept is at once a scientific absurdity and a philosophical monstrosity, and cannot possibly maintain itself in reason. Since a mere time-series is in no sense a causal conception, the causal nexus must be conceived as including End and Means, or it cannot be conceived at all. We repeat, physics alone can never become philosophy; for to start with the *Abstract Machine*, and to proceed with no other principle than the principle of the *Abstract Cause*, is to end with an *Abstract Universe* in ABSOLUTE PLURALISM as the Theory of Being. But Absolute Pluralism is overt repudiation of that *absolute unity in multiplicity* which is the essential aim of all philosophy.

§ 56. What Theory of Being, then, can be logically and philosophically developed out of the Real Machine of anthropology? Briefly, nothing but ABSOLUTE DUALISM. If anthropology aspires to become philosophy, it can climb no higher than THEOLOGICAL ANTHROPOMORPHISM.

Human art cannot originate the materials it works with, but finds them originally given in external Nature. The man is here, the machine is there; even when in active use, the machine acquires no higher spatial unity with the man than that of mere collocation or juxtaposition. For all that anthropology alone can see, the two are absolutely two, not one; it is only from the loftier standpoint of scientific philosophy that a profound underlying oneness of the two comes to light (see §§ 46–48). To anthropology, the machine and its maker or user are fundamentally and unconditionally two, external to each other; and the anthropological concept of the Real Machine is, therefore, an essentially dualistic one.

Now this human dualism of MACHINE AND MAKER, if applied to the formation of a world-theory, can lead only to dualism on a larger scale — to the irredeemably anthropomorphic conception of God and the Universe as essentially external to each other and fundamentally independent of each other. For instance, Descartes, the great Dualist founder of so-called modern philosophy, "beholds the entire universe as a single immense machine, whose wheels and springs were arranged at the beginning, in the simplest manner, by an Eternal Hand" (M. Thomas, *Eloge de Descartes*, crowned by the French Academy in 1765, and prefixed to Cousin's *Œuvres de Descartes*, I. 34). It avails nothing to introduce the principle of "fiat creation," or absolute origination of a universe out of nothing by a mere command; for this principle violates every law of Being and of Thought alike, reconciles no discord, possesses no element of intelligibility, and is absolutely valueless in philosophy. The introduction of it into philosophy (for instance, in the "natural theology" of Butler, Paley, and so many others) has only availed to discredit the principle of teleology itself, and to postpone the development of a truly scientific conception of teleology in Nature.

The anthropological concept of the Real Machine is perfectly valid in anthropology itself; but, when it is applied to philosophy and developed into the cosmological doctrine of ABSOLUTE DUALISM, its fundamental limitations and defects are brought to light in its failure to fulfil the essential philosophical ideal — to discover the principle of *absolute unity in multiplicity*. Dualism is only Pluralism written small — Pluralism reduced to its lowest terms; what tells against the latter tells also, though in a less degree, against the former. Philosophy cannot attain its goal in anthropology; anthropology alone, like physics alone, can never become philosophy.

§ 57. Now, precisely as the Abstract Machine of physics

can become nothing but ABSOLUTE PLURALISM in philosophy, and as the Real Machine of anthropology can become nothing but ABSOLUTE DUALISM in philosophy, so the Real Machine of scientific philosophy can become nothing but ABSOLUTE MONISM.

That the real universe is in some sense *one*, is beyond dispute; the absolute unity of the universe, or, as it is more usually and more loosely phrased, the "uniformity and universality of natural laws," is the necessary presupposition of all scientific investigation. Further, that this one real universe is in some sense a *machine*, has long been a scientific truism. But in what sense? Is it an ARTIFICIAL MACHINE or a NATURAL MACHINE? Anthropological Dualism, applying too literally the analogies of human art, conceives it as an Artificial Machine, and explains it as the "handiwork," not of a natural, but of a supernatural "Maker," a "Great Artificer." But scientific philosophy has shown (see §§ 43-48) that every Artificial Machine is really an ARTIFICIAL AND SEPARABLE ORGAN OF A NATURAL ORGANISM; and it is self-evident that there can be no Natural Organism outside of Nature itself. Hence the universe cannot be an Artificial Machine at all: it can only be a Natural Machine. But the only known Natural Machine is the SELF-MAKING AND SELF-WORKING MACHINE — that is, the REAL ORGANISM. Consequently, if the Universe is a REAL MACHINE at all (and all science proves that it is so), there is no logical escape from the conclusion that it is at the same time a REAL ORGANISM.

§ 58. The case thus far may be briefly summed up as follows: Nature, or the Universe, being by scientific proof and unanimous confession a REAL MACHINE in some sense, the only logical escape from the conclusion that it is the *artificial handiwork* of a supernatural and anthropomorphic ARTIFICER, separate from Nature in space and disparate from Nature in kind or essence, lies in the counter-conclusion that it is the *natural result* of its own self-evolving, self-directing, and self-sustaining IMMANENT ENERGY. There are but three alternatives: (1) the CHAOTIC ABSTRACT UNIVERSE of physics and Absolute Pluralism; (2) the ARTIFICIAL REAL UNIVERSE of anthropology and Absolute Dualism; and (3) the NATURAL REAL UNIVERSE of scientific philosophy and Absolute Monism. Out of these three alternatives (the only possible ones from the standpoint of scientific realism), the third alone is congruous with all human experience, and alone exhibits the legitimate development of the principle of COSMICAL EVOLUTION. The very concept of "evolution" is essentially organic; it is derived from the organism alone, applies to the organism alone, and is utterly meaningless, unless THE INFINITE UNIVERSE IS SCIENTIFICALLY KNOWN AS A REAL ORGANISM-IN-ITSELF. The self-contradictory conjunction of Evolution and Agnosticism in the so-called "philosophy" of the nineteenth century is a mere freak of the hour; for in Agnosticism there is neither acute reasoning nor intrinsic reasonableness — nothing but exploded metaphysics, melancholy misunderstanding, crippling prejudice, confusion of thought, or blank unthinkingness. The philosophy of the future, founded upon the scientific method, must be organic through and through, and build upon the *known organic constitution of the noumenal universe* as the assured result of science itself.

It remains to show that, precisely as the Universe cannot be a REAL MACHINE without being at the same time a REAL ORGANISM, so it cannot be a REAL ORGANISM without being at the same time a REAL PERSON. This will be the subject of the following and concluding paper.

IX.

§ 59. Until the foregoing reasoning has been refuted root and branch, it may without presumption be taken as rationally established that the Infinite Universe is at once a Real Machine and a Real Organism. It remains to show that THE INFINITE UNIVERSE IS AT ONCE A REAL MACHINE, A REAL ORGANISM, AND A REAL PERSON.

§ 60. These three categorical types of Real Being, or three primordial kinds which naturally and necessarily reveal the Supreme Kind of Kinds (see §§ 31–33), are not related to each other as co-ordinate and mutually exclusive species, but rather as successively rising grades of complexity in immanent relational constitution — a conception perfectly familiar in natural science, as illustrated, for example, in Agassiz' *Methods of Study in Natural History* (16th ed. p. 91): "This gradation in [embryological] growth corresponds to the gradation of rank in adult animals, as established upon comparative complexity of structure." In the order of terrestrial evolution, the Machine first appeared as mere matter in motion, then the Organism as plants and animals, and lastly the Person as man; and this order of succession in time corresponds with the gradation of rank in complexity of constitution and with the serial evolution of forms in the scale of being. There is no arbitrary or complete transition: the Organism remains still a Machine, and the Person remains still both Machine and Organism.

§ 61. In the constitution of the Person, therefore, as we know it in ourselves, we find the constitutions of the lower grades or types included and united in a thoroughly harmonious working system. The distinctive feature of the Machine is the mechanical principle of CAUSALITY, as governing the propagation of motion through a material whole of collocated material parts, external one to another; the distinctive feature of the Organism is the principle of FINALITY, as governing the motion and application of organ to function in a constant mediation between the Organism and its organic ends; the distinctive feature of the Person is the principle of conscious self-determination or self-conscious MORALITY, as governing the free formation of ends and means in relation to other selves, and reflexively judging both these ends and their execution through motion in relation to universal rights and duties in a state of society. These three distinctive features of the Machine, the Organism, and the Person are indissolubly united in every human Person as such; the three principles of Causality, Finality, and Morality are all rooted and regnant in the personal constitution, never interfering or colliding with each other in their respective spheres of operation, but harmonizing perfectly in all personal life. If these three principles thus harmonize perfectly in the constitution and life of Man, why may they not, *mutatis mutandis*, harmonize perfectly in the constitution and life of Nature? If Nature is already known to possess the mechanical and the organic constitutions, why may it not possess the personal constitution as well? Nay, if the Thing and the Kind naturally and necessarily reveal each other's essential constitution (see §§ 31–33), and if the Machine and the Organism, as Things, are already proved to reveal the essential constitution of Nature, as their Highest Kind, why is there not a rational necessity that the Person, also, as a higher Thing, shall still more reveal it? Why is it not self-evident that Nature, as ETERNAL ARCHETYPE, necessarily reveals itself in the Machine, the Organism, and the Person, as its primordial ECTYPES in Space and Time? Why is it not self-evident that the Person, which sums up the three in one, is the ECTYPE of ECTYPES,— in a word, that HUMAN NATURE IS THE SUPREME REVELATION OF GOD?

§ 62. These are, at the very least, reasonable questions; and they deserve a very reasonable and respectful answer. Incredible, and even unintelligible, as it may seem at first sight that this boundless system of Nature, this illimitable Universe of Real Being, should be essentially and at bottom ONE INFINITE PERSON, reflection speedily dissipates the swarm of hasty misapprehensions. Images start up of particular machines, organisms, persons; the disparity between these and Nature as a whole is overwhelmingly obvious. Then comes rational meditation, gradually sifting out the essential from the non-essential; and the underlying identity of constitution, the natural revelation of the Kind in the Thing, begins at last to force itself into rational recognition with irresistible power. To conceive the Universe as a Machine is not to imagine it under the form of an enormous steam-engine, but rather to comprehend that the omnipresent causal energy of Nature, producing all motions of matter, whether of masses or of molecules, as dynamical effects, works invariably under the law of Mechanical Causality. To conceive the Universe as an Organism is not to picture it as a gigantic animal, but rather to comprehend that the omnipresent causal-organic energy of Nature, directing all motions of matter, as causal means, to the realization of Nature's eternal end of EVOLUTION, works invariably under the law of Organic Finality. So, too, to conceive the Universe as a Person is not to portray it as a colossal man, but rather to comprehend that the omnipresent causal-organic-personal energy of Nature, being conscious of itself and its own eternal end of SELF-EVOLUTION THROUGH SELF-INVOLUTION, and executing this end through the successive and gradual creation of FINITE MACHINES, FINITE ORGANISMS, AND FINITE SELVES WITHIN ITS OWN INFINITE SELF, works invariably under the law of Ideal Morality. It is impracticable here to unfold these thoughts in full; they are now barely hinted at, in order to clear the way for a thoughtful and unprejudiced consideration of the thesis that the Universe is, and must be, a Real Person.

§ 63. The Finite Artificial Machine, or artificial organ constructed by a natural organism, is external in space both to the constructor, or user, and to the effect which it is constructed to produce; it mediates between the two as a causal means outside of both, as, for instance, the chisel between the sculptor and the statue, or the printing-press between the printer and the book, or the army between the conqueror and his conquest. It is owing to this constitutional externality in space that physics can so easily conceive the Abstract Machine — can so easily, in abstract thought, make a pseudo-separation between the two elements of cause and effect, on the one hand, and of end and means, on the other; for both the preconceived end in the mind of the maker and the realized end in the material world are equally external to the Machine as a mediator between the two, and what separates them, yet links them together, is the mediating chain of physical causes and effects in the motions of the Machine itself. Hence physics can readily disregard both preconceived and realized ends, and confine itself exclusively to mere motion and its laws; and hence, too, the legitimacy and utility of the Abstract Machine as a physical concept, which serves to simplify, and thereby helps to solve, purely mechanical problems.

But, in the case of the Universe as an Infinite Natural Machine, no such externality in space obtains, and no such abstraction of the causal from the final relation is possible at all, unless the Abstract Universe is recognized as necessarily implying the Real Universe from which to abstract it. The Real Universe, as a Real Natural Machine, must be absolutely all-inclusive; both causal and final relations, inseparable in the complete constitution of every Real Machine, must be strictly and wholly within the all-inclusive Universe; there can be here neither external maker nor external effect — both maker and effect must be internal only. In other words, if the Infinite Universe is a Real Machine at all, it must be, not merely a Real Machine, but also a Self-Making and Self-Working Real Machine — that is, a Real Organism: THE INFINITE UNIVERSE CANNOT BE A REAL MACHINE WITHOUT BEING A REAL ORGANISM, TOO. If the principles and premises of scientific realism are sound, the argument here is more than probable — it is demonstrative.

§ 64. Now precisely as stringent a rational necessity inheres in the next step of the argument: namely, that the Infinite Universe cannot be a Real Organism without being a Real Person, too.

The Finite Natural Organism, or Real Machine constructed by Nature, is both *Cause and Effect of Itself* and *End and Means to Itself*: it is the *Self-Making and Self-Working Machine* (§ 47). This is no new conception; it was foreshadowed in Aristotle's well-known doctrine of the soul as an "entelecheia," and fully developed in Kant's profound analysis of the Organism as a "Naturzweck" — a natural whole in which whole and parts are reciprocally Cause and Effect, End and Means (*Kritik der Urtheilskraft*, §§ 65, 66). But Kant overlooked another essential characteristic of the Organism which is even more profoundly significant and instructive. He failed to analyze its Total Organic End as two-fold: (1) as INDWELLING OR IMMANENT END, and (2) as OUTGOING OR EXIENT END. The Immanent End of the Organism is SELF-EVOLUTION, partly recognized in the common proverb that "self-preservation is the first law of Nature": this Kant saw. But the Exient End is SELF-DEVOTION — devotion of self to the preservation and evolution of the higher self or species, to which the individual Organism is related as the organ or organic cell is related to the Organism itself: this Kant did not see. Nevertheless, this principle of the Exient End (clearly illustrated in the reproductive system) unites the individual Organism to its kind as a larger and inclusive Organism, unites this in turn, as a new individual, to a higher kind, and so on indefinitely. Thus the Exient End appears as a teleological principle of unity and intelligibility throughout the whole of Nature. The Immanent End gives to the Organism no "Others," but merely its "Self"; the Exient End gives to it "External Others," or a higher self in a NOT-SELF, as a separate, but normally necessary, complement to its own being. These two equally essential elements of the Total Organic End are equally wrought into the very warp and woof of the organic constitution itself.

But, in the case of the Universe as the Infinite Natural Organism, the Total Organic End ceases to be dualistically separable as literally Immanent and Exient, inasmuch as the Infinite can have *no* "External Others." The principle of Immanency and Exiency, notwithstanding, remains in the strictly monistic distinction between *Self as One Whole* (principle of Self-Evolution) and *Self as Many Parts or Internal Others* (principle of Self-Devotion); just as the Finite Natural Organism exists as One Organism of Many Organs or Cells, in which each alike, organism and cell, not only lives its own true life unsubverted and uninfringed by that of the other, but also devotes its own real life to that of the other. Hence, in the Infinite, Self and Not-Self are numerically identical. But Numerical Identity of Self and Not-Self, Subject and Object, constitutes the UNITY OF SELF-CONSCIOUSNESS IN THE PERSON. Consequently, THE INFINITE UNIVERSE CANNOT BE A REAL ORGANISM WITHOUT BEING A REAL PERSON, TOO.

Thus we are led to discover the LAW OF THE CORRELAtion and Ultimate Identity of all Real Types in the Person.

§ 65. The same momentous conclusion, forced upon us above by studying the constitutions of the Machine and the Organism as *concrete realities*, is no less forced upon us by studying the laws of Causality and Finality as their *real principles*.

The idea of all Force or Might in Nature being confessedly derived, even in physics, from human experience of Conscious Effort, these inevitable consequences follow from §§ 51–55: —

I. The Efficient or Out-Making Cause necessarily contains within itself the Preconceived End; the Effect or Out-Made Result necessarily contains within itself the Realized End; and the Causal Bond is itself the Energetic Realizing End in Effort.

II. Therefore, the principle of Efficient or Mechanical Causality necessarily contains within itself the principle of Organic Finality.

Similarly, the idea of all Right in Nature being derived from human experience of Conscience, these inevitable consequences follow from § 64: —

1. The Immanent Organic End is Self-Evolution, or Ethical Egoism; the Exient Organic End is Self-Devotion, or Ethical Altruism; and the Total Organic End is Harmony of Ethical Egoism and Ethical Altruism in Character.

II. The lower Finite Organism realizes its Character, of which Nature is conscious, in Ethical Unconsciousness; the higher Finite Organism realizes its Character in Ethical Consciousness of Limited Freedom; the Infinite Organism of Nature realizes its Character in Ethical Consciousness of Illimitable Freedom.

III. Therefore, the principle of Organic Finality necessarily contains within itself the principle of FREEDOM, SELF-DETERMINATION, OR IDEAL MORALITY.

§ 66. This magnificent result, that *Causality involves Finality and Finality involves Morality,*— in other words, that the three supreme and constitutive principles of the Real Universe are at bottom one, from the heliocentric point of view, in the one principle of ABSOLUTE PERSONALITY,— is analogous to the vast modern generalizations (1) that all forms of Matter are at bottom one in IDENTITY OF SUBSTANCE, (2) that all manifestations of Force are at bottom one in IDENTITY OF ENERGY, and (3) that all stages of cosmical change are at bottom one in IDENTITY OF EVOLUTIONARY PROCESS. To these it adds (1) that all immanent relational constitutions, whether of machine, organism, or person, are at bottom one, in the personal constitution, in IDENTITY OF ESSENCE, and (2) that all natural laws are at bottom one in IDENTITY OF PRINCIPLE. It therefore constitutes the crowning discovery of the Scientific Method, necessary to complete the demonstration of Absolute Monism, in the LAW OF THE CORRELATION AND ULTIMATE IDENTITY OF ALL REAL PRINCIPLES IN PERSONALITY. Who could overestimate the value or importance of such a result? The ultimately inevitable scientific identification of all physical, biological, and psychological forces, as universally correlated and mutually convertible forms of one eternal and omnipresent Force, means, in the light of this transcendently sublime law, not the degradation of all forces to the level of blind mechanical necessity, but the elevation of all forces to the height of intelligent spiritual freedom. This is the natural and unforced evolution of Science itself, through the philosophized Scientific Method, into the PHILOSOPHY OF FREE RELIGION.

§ 67. In this way it is made clear, to any one who has capacity to comprehend and patience to master the argument, that the Infinite Universe cannot be a Real Machine without being a Real Organism, and cannot be a Real Organism without being a Real Person; and that this philosophical last conclusion is just as certain as the scientific first premise that the Universe is indeed a Machine. This, then, in briefest form, is the SCIENTIFIC WORLD-CONCEPTION, as Absolute Monism or Scientific Theism: —

MECHANICAL CAUSALITY, *or the Law of Motion*, ORGANIC FINALITY, *or the Law of Life, and* IDEAL MORALITY, *or the Law of Holiness, Justice, and Love,*— *the three eternal and all-pervasive Real Principles by which the whole known Universe exists,*— *are at bottom* ONE *in the Real Principle of Omnipresent Self-Conscious Energy or* ABSOLUTE PERSONALITY, *and constitute the* UNITY OF THE UNIVERSE IN THE ESSENTIAL BEING AND LIFE OF GOD, AS AT ONCE INFINITE MACHINE, INFINITE ORGANISM, AND INFINITE PERSON.

§ 68. Whatever higher truth lies unrevealed in the boundless mystery of the Unknown, this *Truth of the Known* stands fast as the eternal foundation of the Real Universe. If any one should contemn the idea of the ALL-PERSON, thus conceived, how meanly, alas, must he think of moral personality itself — how blindly must he despise the dignity, the majesty, the sublimity of his own nature as MAN!

§ 69. REAL PERSONALITY, finite and relative in Man, infinite and absolute in Nature, is thus the last word of Science and Philosophy — the first word of Ethics and Religion; for Man's moral nature is necessarily rooted and included in his personal nature, and his personal nature is necessarily rooted and included in that of the ALL which it dimly, yet supremely, reveals. There is no other central unifying principle, whether in thought or in action, whether in the life of the individual or in the life of society, by which the Real may be known or the Ideal may be embodied. There is no other central unifying principle by which Man may develop or reform either himself or society, or by which the all-divinizing Enthusiasm of Humanity may be kindled in his soul, or by which the world may be redeemed from its mountain-load of injustice, suffering, and sin. Think highly, think reverently, think devotedly, O brother-men, of that MORAL IDEAL which is the very core, law, and life of your own personality, and which could be to you no law of august, all-commanding obligation, of transcendent and eternal authority, were it not identical with the innermost LAW OF NATURE by which the planets roll, the sun shines, the Universe itself exists. For that divine passion for the FINITE IDEAL which makes the hero, the reformer, the prophet, the saint, is but a spark of that eternal and ethereal fire which burns at the very heart of Being, and keeps God himself true to his own INFINITE IDEAL.

§ 70. That thus the ultimate ground of all Art, Science, Philosophy, Ethics, and Religion, in strict accordance with the Scientific Method, is proved to lie in the immanent relational constitution of the Supreme Genus-in-Itself, or Real Universe, as Absolute Divine Person,— that this innermost nature of the known Cosmos as All-Person is most profoundly revealed in the distinctively personal, ethical, or spiritual nature of Man,— that "Man's Place in Nature" is that of a free and loyal SERVANT OF THE DIVINE IDEAL, and that all his duties, hopes, joys, loves, aspirations, activities, destinies, depend upon his discovering intelligently and fulfilling freely the exact function in Nature and in Human Society which this unalterable Divine relationship assigns to him,— these things will explain themselves to the quick-witted, and cannot be amplified or emphasized now.

§ 71. The time has come to close this series of papers, which is merely a partial prospectus of what may be hoped to find hereafter a more appropriate place and a far better form. Its aim has been to show the way out of Agnosticism into the sunlight of the predestined Philosophy of Science. The labor of writing these too closely packed articles will be well repaid, if here and there some thoughtful spirit has caught even a glimpse of the sublime vistas of truth waiting to be revealed to mankind by the philosophic use of the Scientific Method. Said Ralph Waldo Emerson, America's greatest prophet: "There is a statement of religion possible which makes all skepticism absurd." Is there not such a statement lying latent and implicit in the PHILOSOPHY OF FREE RELIGION?

PRESS NOTICES

OF

SCIENTIFIC THEISM.

THE work is, we think, an important addition to the literature of the subject. It treats of Theism from a new point of view, and by means of original methods. The treatise is, in a certain sense, original. . . . In its polemic against Phenomenism and its assertion of Realism, it opens up a discussion of the utmost importance. . . . It is evident that, in this argument, Dr. Abbot is right, and the idealists and sensists wrong. . . . A book as full of thought as this furnishes innumerable topics for inquiry and criticism. If every position taken by Dr. Abbot cannot be maintained, his book remains an original contribution to philosophy of a high order and of great value. — *Dr. James Freeman Clarke, in the Unitarian Review.*

This is a notable book. It is notable both for what it is and for what it indicates, namely, returning health and sanity in philosophic thought. . . . Whatever one may think of the position in which the argument of "Scientific Theism" culminates, one cannot but be impressed with the deep insight, the clear intellect, the moral fervor of the author. Whoever has the interests of philosophy at heart will welcome this masterly attempt to effect a reconciliation between philosophy and modern science. No thorough-going idealist, to be sure, will be satisfied with a book which so powerfully assails his fundamental positions. . . . We cannot but be thankful for this strong and well-reasoned protest against the agnosticism so current in our times. — *Prof. H. A. P. Torrey, in the Andover Review.*

The phrase "Scientific Theism" expresses in itself a subject of great interest. We do not so much wish to write a careful review of Dr. Abbot's very vigorous work as to discuss in connection with it the topic brought forward by it. This discussion will be guided by the view presented by Dr. Abbot. The strong assertion of Realism with which the book opens we heartily accept, with this slight exception, that the author seems to us to lay undue emphasis on the unfortunate effects of

Nominalism in preparing the way for Idealism. . . . These quotations are perhaps sufficient to give the central idea of Dr. Abbot, the one we wish to consider,—that the universe is an organism animate in every part with the inbiding Divine Presence. It is very plain that this conception furnishes to the mind of the author—it may also to many other minds—a very quickening spiritual interpretation of the world, bringing his thoughts and feelings in close contact with God. Every portion of the book makes this very plain.—*Ex-President John Bascom, in the New Englander and Yale Review.*

In thus calling attention to the Nominalistic current in philosophical thought, and tracing it from its source to its latest issues, Mr. Abbot has done a real service. The justice of his complaint must also be allowed, that the significance of the Nominalistic principle has not hitherto been appreciated by the historians of philosophy. Further, his detection of a Nominalistic vein in Kant is just and important. . . . This vindication of the objective standpoint of science and this account of the real nature of the distinction between the noumenon and phenomenon are excellent. The principle of "Relationism," if properly understood, is undeniably true, and must supersede all merely "subjective" principles. — *Prof. James Seth, in Mind.*

Ces ouvrages de quatre philosophes contemporains, dont deux, ou peutêtre trois, appartiennent à l'Amérique, et un à la Russie, représentent de remarquables efforts de construction métaphysique et morale dus à des penseurs indépendants et profonds qui ont reçu diversement l'influence des doctrines en conflit à notre époque : positivisme, matérialisme, idéalisme, pessimisme, évolutionisme, et se sont fait des croyances philosophiques en dehors de toute école. . . . Le système de M. Abbot est une espèce du genre *positivisme*, en ce qu'il prend dans la science les fondements de la philosophie ; mais cette espèce diffère des autres, ou des plus connues, par le caractère affirmatif de ses conclusions sur des points de métaphysique au sujet desquels le positivisme, à son début, professait l'ignorance invincible et prétendait observer la neutralité en refusant d'examiner. — *M. Renouvier, in La Critique Philosophique.*

Un penseur américain très distingué, M. Francis Ellingwood Abbot, a combattu avec une grande force, dans un ouvrage récent, la théorie de l'Inconnaissable, et esquissé une sorte de religion scientifique qui nous parait un heureux amendement à celle de M. Spencer. L'exposé sommaire de sa doctrine servira de complément assez naturel à celui du précédent système. . . . La pensée de M. Abbot m'a paru assez profonde et assez originale pour mériter d'être reproduite littéralement. Le *Théisme Scientifique* est, depuis les stoïciens, la plus hardie tentative pour faire de l'univers un Dieu revêtu de justice, de bonté, de moralité.

M. Abbot va même plus loin que le stoïcisme : il fait de l'univers une personne. Ce qui donne à son système un intérêt et une importance exceptionnels, c'est, nous l'avons dit, qu'il se présente comme une application rigoureuse de la méthode qui a conduit la science à de si merveilleux résultats. — *M. Ludovic Carrau, in La Philosophie Religieuse en Angleterre (Paris : Félix Alcan, 1888).*

Mr. Abbot has presented us with a brilliant and enticing argument, and many who, after a careful reading and study of his book, still feel themselves compelled to hesitate and wait, will admit its strong persuasiveness and charm ; while others will doubtless be induced through its means to abandon at once their old agnostic doubts. — *Chicago University.*

These lofty and valuable conclusions he obtains by a process of reasoning which is in the main sound, and founded upon sound premises. The book, as we have said, must take an honorable place in the literature of the subject. — *Boston Literary World.*

Dr. F. E. Abbot's new book, the "Science of Theism," confirms the opinion of the few best able to judge that he is the ablest philosophical thinker in America, and that his work seems to be the foundation of that deeper religion of the future, sure to come, which will satisfy both the head and the heart of man. — *Boston Sunday Herald, editorial.*

This work, by one of the first living minds, is a profound attempt to place theism on the immovable ground of modern science. — *Montreal Star.*

Although offered as but a sketch of the most prominent features of the "Philosophy of Science," Dr. Abbot's exposition in his Part I. is so comprehensive, so critical and scholarly, and so suggestive, that he may find, as Darwin did when he brought out the "Origin of Species" as preliminary to a great work, that he has done enough already to found a school of investigation and to establish himself as the master of a new departure, profoundly original and significant, in the highest form of research. — *Boston Transcript.*

Since the immortal treatises of Darwin himself, which have been so grievously misunderstood, we have not had a treatise which meets so well the demands of all science and all religion as does Dr. Abbot's "Theism." He does explicitly and positively what Darwin did by implication. The great Darwin gave us the right method of studying visible Nature ; Dr. Abbot extends the theory and method to the universe, to the human mind, to God. Such a book should make an epoch in the intellectual history of our country. The book is a very great performance. — *Boston Beacon.*

Dr. Abbot has come forward with a discussion of the problem that is destined to make an epoch in the world of thought, — a discussion which, as the result of twenty-five years of consecutive thinking, is marked by such masterly grasp of the whole issue, and such clearness of analysis and reconstructive power in dealing with it, that no thoughtful man or woman can afford to pass it by. . . . Only once in a great while does a work of such moment appear. . . . For many years now powerful intellects have turned away from the realms of theology, once haunted by such minds as those of Dante, Thomas Aquinas, and Pascal; but of the fact that in this little book there are laid the foundations of what may again dower the barren and prosaic world with sublime theologies, the work of grand and sanely imaginative intellects, there can be little question. — *Rev. Francis Tiffany, in the Boston Herald.*

It bears evidence throughout of wide reading and close thinking: every page throbs with brain-force. . . . He has a fervent faith that right thinking is necessary to right feeling and right action; and that religion, in order to be redeemed from the effeminate sentimentalism and empty ceremony into which it has in modern times so largely fallen, must come again under the sway, as in previous epochs of the world, of a robust system of thought. This necessary system of thought, he believes, is furnished by science and the scientific method; and to prove this position is, in general, the theme and motive of his book. . . . Whatever might be said on some of the special points of Mr. Abbot's argument, his book starts from the right ground, and proceeds by the right method, and reaches essentially the right end. It is a masterful treatment of its high theme, and can but have great weight toward the establishing of the religious philosophy that is to come as the product of science, — of science in its large sense, as applied to the whole universe of matter and mind. . . . It has science at its back, and, with that support, its leading ideas will, we believe, eventually win the battle. . . . The larger book, of which the preface to this hints, we earnestly hope may yet come. But, even if it does not, this one just as it is, notwithstanding these minor defects, deserves not only a kind, but a proud, welcome from all lovers of high and free thinking on great themes. — *Rev. William J. Potter, in the Boston Index.*

There could hardly be a greater opposition than that of such a scheme as this to such a scheme as that which is furnished by Mr. Frederic Harrison, when he says: " For all that we know to the contrary, man is the creator of the order and harmony of the universe, for he has imagined it." Spencer, who disagrees with Harrison so much concerning the nature of religion, agrees with him perfectly in this, and they both agree with Kant. Dr. Abbot's theory is therefore a new departure of commanding interest and importance. ... At a time when "Retreat upon Kant" is so generally the philosophic order for the day, it is certainly invigorating and refreshing to hear this voice of manly opposition; and it does not seem to me by any means impossible that we have seen with our eyes a man from whom will date another epoch in philosophy, bright with such faith and hope as have not been upon the earth since Parker gave to Kant's abstractions the positive warmth and color of his individual genius for religion. — *Rev. J. W. Chadwick, in the Brooklyn Union.*

No one need resort to mere compliments in expressing very great admiration of the argument here set forth, if not entire assent. The few who know Dr. Abbot as a speculative thinker expect, when they open this book, more than they could justly expect from any other American philosopher. They look for the evidence of thorough training in the "discipline" of philosophy, and of a wide and deep knowledge of the masters of thought, which have yet not been able to overburden or destroy a natural metaphysical ability of the purest strain. They look for clearness and exactness of expression, the virtues commonly deemed most alien to metaphysics. They look for a vigorous exposure of the idols of the hour, and, above all, for the most substantial constructive work. These things are all found here, and we trust that the few will become a multitude. Dr. Abbot has the one quality which should command the attention, at least, of the many: he is an intense believer. He has faith in natural science, which, indeed, is in no lack of devotees today; and he has as much faith in religion, which has now no superabundance of real friends; and his two faiths are thoroughly one. ... Realistic evolution will inevitably triumph over all other theories. But there are two forms of it, the mechanical and the organic; and in the establishment of the profounder, the organic, view Dr. Abbot puts forth all his strength in what must be considered the most satisfactory chapter of the book. His analysis of the idea of machinery, and his exposure of its glaring insufficiency to account for the life and growth of the universe, are extremely cogent. ... We cannot deny the necessary revolution in philosophy which Scientific Realism, as here stated, should effect. We hope it will soon come, and that Dr. Abbot will receive for this book, and larger books hereafter, the just meed of his very high deserts as a philosopher. ... "Scientific Theism" is one of the great books of our generation. — *Rev. N. P. Gilman, in the Christian Register.*

Dr. Abbot has confined his essay to two hundred and twenty pages, which are crammed with strong, vigorous thought. ... This book clears away much confusion and error, and it seems to us the most valuable contribution to the philosophy of religion yet made. . . . Dr. Abbot has done a grand work, which must have an important effect on the religious thought of the present century. — *Omaha Republican.*

In his rejection of agnosticism, Mr. Abbot is the strongest antagonist Herbert Spencer has yet met with, and he is quite competent to enter into combat with a thinker so able. . . . His book is one of the ablest which has recently appeared in behalf of science. It is well calculated to work a new revolution in the doctrine of evolution, and to work out the philosophy based upon it in a deeper and surer manner than ever before. It must attract attention everywhere for its close reasoning and for its breadth of philosophic grasp on the problems involved. The author manifests a power of philosophic insight which has been denied to such men as Herbert Spencer. — *Rev. George W. Cooke, in the New York Day Star.*

It is a strongly characterized and scholarly piece of work, doing honor to American thought; and it is much to be desired that the world should see the system developed in its entirety. — *Prof. C. L. Peirce, in the New York Nation.*

We are not usually much attracted by books on scientific theism. Too commonly they are attempts to make use of the general interest in science to call attention to some not very original or profound speculations about religion. The result often is a syncretism of poor science and worse theology. Such a prejudice cannot attach itself to any work from the pen of Mr. Abbot. Many of us remember his striking article on "Space and Time," published in the "North American Review" in 1864, which, as he tells us, was partly the germ of the present work. That article showed such philosophic insight and originality, and such a grasp of the question, as to lead us to hope for further discussions of the same quality. Our wish is at last gratified in the small but very valuable treatise before us. — *Boston Daily Advertiser.*

Dr. Abbot's scheme of thought has a decided claim to recognition as a striking contribution to current philosophy. — *London Academy.*

We even doubt whether any human being could come to real belief in God by this road. We do not intend by this to suggest that the work done by Mr. Abbot is badly done or is unnecessary. It is neither. It is well done, and it is necessary to be done; for it is very desirable that the clever philosophical agnostic should be taken on his own ground, and pushed into a corner. Any one who wants to see this done should read Mr. Abbot's book. — *London Inquirer.*

This one thing Dr. Abbot seems to us to have done: he has made Herbert Spencer's doctrine of the "Unknowable" antiquated. It has passed into the realm of the obsolete and the nonsensical. . . . To us, then, the great achievement of the book is the clear statement and demonstration of the scientific method as applied to the external world, and its application to the problems of philosophy. . . . We hesitate to say of all what we gladly say of the "ground principle": that being established, the rest will come; and it will come the sooner and the safer because this one man has patiently wrestled with the problem for twenty years, and is willing now to devote the remainder of his life to the consideration of the questions involved in the hopes of the human heart. Such praise, inadequate as it may seem, is what few men in a generation deserve. — *Rev. George Batchelor, in the Unitarian Review.*

www.ingramcontent.com/pod-product-compliance
Lightning Source LLC
Chambersburg PA
CBHW020302090426
42735CB00009B/1188